'An accurate history and nuanced analysis of nuclear weapons' impact on global politics – accessible and insightful for experts and non-experts alike.'
**Carlotta Minnella,
European University Institute**

'Understanding nuclear weapons is absolutely essential if we are to prevent their future use. This book does an excellent job of bringing clarity to an increasingly difficult problem.'
**Andrew Futter,
University of Leicester**

'Shamai's exhaustive, balanced and timely analysis reminds us that the most destructive weapons ever built may still be what keeps peace alive.'
**Lana Obradovic,
University of Nebraska Omaha**

'A rich and thought-provoking read on a subject that 80 years on from the atomic bombings of Hiroshima and Nagasaki, remains as relevant as ever.'
**Nicola Leveringhaus,
King's College London**

'A must-read for those who research and study deterrence! Patricia Shamai provides us with a detailed historical account of nuclear weapon use and reputation.'
**Michelle Black,
University of Nebraska Omaha**

The status quo is broken. The world is grappling with a web of challenges that could threaten our very existence. If we believe in a better world, now is the time to question the purpose behind our actions and those taken in our name.

Enter the What Is It For? series – a bold exploration of the core elements shaping our world, from religion and free speech to animal rights and war. This series cuts through the noise to reveal the true impact of these topics, what they really do and why they matter.

Ditching the usual heated debates and polarizations, this series offers fresh, forward-thinking insights. Leading experts present groundbreaking ideas and point to ways forward for real change, urging us to envision a brighter future.

Each book dives into the history and function of its subject, uncovering its role in society and, crucially, how it can be better.

Series editor: George Miller

Visit **bristoluniversitypress.co.uk/what-is-it-for** to find out more about the series.

Available now

WHAT ARE ANIMAL RIGHTS FOR?
Steve Cooke

WHAT IS COUNTERTERRORISM FOR?
Leonie Jackson

WHAT IS CYBERSECURITY FOR?
Tim Stevens

WHAT IS DRUG POLICY FOR?
Julia Buxton

WHAT IS HISTORY FOR?
Robert Gildea

WHAT IS HUMANISM FOR?
Richard Norman

WHAT IS JOURNALISM FOR?
Jon Allsop

WHAT IS THE MONARCHY FOR?
Laura Clancy

WHAT ARE MUSEUMS FOR?
Jon Sleigh

WHAT ARE NUCLEAR WEAPONS FOR?
Patricia Shamai

WHAT ARE THE OLYMPICS FOR?
Jules Boykoff

WHAT IS PHILANTHROPY FOR?
Rhodri Davies

WHAT ARE PRISONS FOR?
Hindpal Singh Bhui

WHAT IS TRUTH FOR?
N.J. Enfield

WHAT IS VEGANISM FOR?
Catherine Oliver

WHAT IS WAR FOR?
Jack McDonald

WHAT IS THE WELFARE STATE FOR?
Paul Spicker

WHAT ARE ZOOS FOR?
Heather Browning and Walter Veit

Forthcoming

WHAT IS ANARCHISM FOR?
Nathan Jun

WHAT IS ANTHROPOLOGY FOR?
Kriti Kapila

WHAT ARE CONSPIRACY THEORIES FOR?
James Fitzgerald

WHAT IS FIFA FOR?
Alan Tomlinson

WHAT IS FREE SPEECH FOR?
Gavan Titley

WHAT IS IMMIGRATION POLICY FOR?
Madeleine Sumption

WHAT IS INTERNATIONAL DEVELOPMENT FOR?
Andrea Cornwall

WHAT ARE MARKETS FOR?
Phillip Roscoe

WHAT IS MUSIC FOR?
Fleur Brouwer

WHAT ARE THE POLICE FOR?
Ben Bradford

WHAT IS RELIGION FOR?
Malise Ruthven

WHAT IS RESILIENCE FOR?
Hamideh Mahdiani

WHAT IS SPACE EXPLORATION FOR?
Tony Milligan and Koji Tachibana

WHAT ARE STATUES FOR?
Milly Williamson

PATRICIA SHAMAI is Principal Lecturer in International Relations and Associate Head of School in the Faculty of Humanities and Social Sciences at the University of Portsmouth.

WHAT ARE NUCLEAR WEAPONS FOR?

PATRICIA SHAMAI

First published in Great Britain in 2026 by

Bristol University Press
University of Bristol
1–9 Old Park Hill
Bristol
BS2 8BB
UK
t: +44 (0)117 374 6645
e: bup-info@bristol.ac.uk

Details of international sales and distribution partners are available at
bristoluniversitypress.co.uk

© Patricia Shamai 2026

British Library Cataloguing in Publication Data
A catalogue record for this book is available from the British Library

ISBN 978-1-5292-3417-6 paperback
ISBN 978-1-5292-3418-3 ePub
ISBN 978-1-5292-3419-0 ePdf

The right of Patricia Shamai to be identified as author of this work has been
asserted by her in accordance with the Copyright, Designs and Patents Act 1988.

All rights reserved: no part of this publication may be reproduced, stored in
a retrieval system, or transmitted in any form or by any means, electronic,
mechanical, photocopying, recording, or otherwise without the prior permission of
Bristol University Press.

Every reasonable effort has been made to obtain permission to reproduce
copyrighted material. If, however, anyone knows of an oversight, please contact
the publisher.

The statements and opinions contained within this publication are solely those of the
author and not of the University of Bristol or Bristol University Press. The University
of Bristol and Bristol University Press disclaim responsibility for any injury to
persons or property resulting from any material published in this publication.

Bristol University Press works to counter discrimination on grounds of gender,
race, disability, age and sexuality.

Cover design: Tom Appshaw

Bristol University Press' authorised representative in the European
Union is: Easy Access System Europe, Mustamäe tee 50, 10621
Tallinn, Estonia, Email: gpsr.requests@easproject.com

CONTENTS

List of Figures		xii
Acknowledgements		xiv
Preface		xv
1.	**Introduction**	1
2.	**Origins**	18
3.	**The Cold War**	37
4.	**Taboos and Stigmas**	48
5.	**Non-Proliferation, Arms Control and Popular Protest**	67
6.	**After the Cold War**	88
7.	**9/11 and the Nuclear Threat**	106
8.	**Conclusion**	128
Notes		143
Further Reading		159
Index		161

LIST OF FIGURES

1.1 The first atomic bombing of Hiroshima, Japan, by B-29 Superfortresses, 6 August 1945. US Army, AAF photograph. Photo number: A-58914. Library of Congress, Prints and Photographs Division, Washington, DC — 2

3.1 Estimated global nuclear warhead stockpiles, 1945–2024 — 43

4.1 Mushroom cloud with ships below during Operation Crossroads nuclear weapons test on Bikini Atoll, July 1946. Photograph, Ira Eaker papers (1917–89). Library of Congress, Prints and Photographs Division, Washington, DC — 62

5.1 Anti-war, anti-nuclear-weapons rally, Wall Street, New York, US, 1981. Photograph by Bernard Gotfryd. Bernard Gotfryd photograph collection, Library of Congress, Prints and Photographs Division, Washington, DC — 83

7.1 Estimated global nuclear warhead inventories, 2025. Hans M. Kristensen, Matt Korda, Robert S. Norris, Eliana Johns and Mackenzie Knight (Federation of American Scientists) — 121

LIST OF FIGURES

8.1 Nuclear intercontinental ballistic missiles, Victory Day parade, Moscow, 2024. Photograph by Vadim Savitsky. Ministry of Defence of the Russian Federation (reproduced under Creative Commons Attribution 4.0 licence)   136

ACKNOWLEDGEMENTS

Special thanks to my editor George Miller at Bristol University Press for setting this book in motion and for his support, patience and encouragement throughout the writing process. Thanks also to the Bristol University Press team, especially Ellen Mitchell. Any errors or omissions in the book are entirely my own.

I would also like to thank my colleagues at the University of Portsmouth, in particular, Dr Melita Lazell, Dr Nora Siklodi, Dr Laura Hyman, Professor Angela Crack, Dr Joseph Burridge, Professor Peter Lee and Professor Anne Murphy. Inspiration has also come from my good friends Joel Davies, Julie Sapphire and Colonel Douglas W. Warnock Jr.

Finally, none of my passion and interest in this subject could have occurred without the support of my family, to whom my gratitude is immeasurable.

PREFACE

It's a cold, rainy Saturday afternoon in Winchester and I'm in my favourite coffee shop. It's full of fresh-faced students chatting about their plans for the weekend and the dramas of the night before. Young families are shaking rain off their coats and discussing the menu. As I wait for a friend, I glance at my phone: *'Breaking news … Putin puts Russia's nuclear forces on "special alert"'*. Russian troops, having invaded Ukraine, have now crossed the southern border to attack the capital, Kyiv. My heart sinks. It's 2022. We've barely come out of the COVID-19 pandemic. Life was just getting back to normal.

To many analysts, nuclear weapons seemed a relic of the past. A handful of states have them, but the consensus was that they would never be used as new technologies and threats now overshadowed them. But now here was Putin making the nuclear threat pressing once again. Nuclear weapons, it seemed, were back.

I know the deadly, catastrophic effects of nuclear weapons. I have written, researched and taught about them for the past 15 years. I look away from the news to see the students on the table in front of me and think how young they are, so full of energy and dreams. I think about the generations before them, those that fought and survived the Second World War, those that joined Campaign for Nuclear Disarmament marches, and those that lived through the fall of the Berlin Wall. I think of my own generation, witnessing first-hand the events of 9/11, living with the threat of terrorism and adapting to the internet revolution. How have nuclear weapons affected our lives? Have they been a force to prevent war? Or a tool of brutality and devastation? Why are they still relevant today? What ultimately are nuclear weapons *for*?

In this book, I argue that the purpose of nuclear weapons is primarily to stop war. This may seem odd, as these are the deadliest of weapons with the potential to destroy the world. This very quality makes them a strategic deterrent, the ultimate tools of hard power. Nuclear weapons provide states with a political advantage over other non-nuclear weapon states, enabling them to shape events in their favour. The flip side of this is that this power brings moral responsibility. Fear of a loss of status, exclusion and condemnation has, to date, deterred even the most hostile of states. The moral reaction to nuclear weapons among the public and politicians has led to international efforts to control and eliminate this threat, and also provoked efforts to address broader humanitarian and environmental concerns.

How the world has seen the importance and relevance of nuclear weapons, and how world leaders have been influenced by the fear of nuclear war, has changed over time, in line with the ebb and flow of social and ideological global trends. Nuclear weapons are barbaric methods of warfare, yet some states are racing to acquire them. No state with nuclear weapons is willing to give them up. In fact, nuclear weapon states are spending billions to modernize their capability. The world knows the damaging effects such weapons could cause, either through deliberate use or accidental damage, yet states still develop programmes to produce nuclear energy. Perplexing as nuclear weapons are, they are, for now, the ultimate weapons until another invention challenges them.

As I think of the importance nuclear weapons have on our lives, I decide to write this book to share my ideas. Three years later, this is the outcome. As the final preparations are made for this book to go to print, sadly, the war has not ended in Ukraine. The nuclear threat remains as intense today as ever before. Israel and America, concerned by the extent of Iran's nuclear capability, have launched military strikes on suspected nuclear weapons facilities in Iran. The book is written to challenge the reader to consider the complexities of the nuclear puzzle and to appreciate the significance of the nuclear threat today.

1
INTRODUCTION

On 28 January 2025, the Doomsday clock inched closer to midnight, moving from 90 to 89 seconds to the hour. The time on the clock, a device designed by members of the Bulletin of Atomic Scientists, has been published each year since 1947. Its purpose is to warn the world how close we are to global destruction caused by manmade technologies, and in particular, 'the greatest threat to humanity', nuclear weapons.[1] The closer the hands get to midnight, the closer the scientists reckon we are to disaster. It is, they say, a 'metaphor – a reminder of the perils we must address if we are to remain on the planet'.

Nuclear weapons have only been used on two occasions, both in 1945. US President Harry S. Truman authorized the first use of the bomb on 25 July 1945. On 6 August 1945, US B-29 Superfortress bombers flew over the Japanese city of Hiroshima and, at 08:15 local time, a 15-kiloton bomb (equivalent to 15,000 tons of TNT) was detonated approximately

Figure 1.1: The first atomic bombing of Hiroshima, Japan, by B-29 Superfortresses, 6 August 1945

1,900 feet above the city. The effect was catastrophic. One eyewitness recalled:

> Suddenly, a great orange flame engulfed the side of our house, and set the shoji walls on fire. As I instinctively walked toward the kitchen for water, the tatami floors gave out from under me and I cowered over underneath the house as debris began to fall on my head. Moments later,

> it became eerily quiet. 'Meguchan, meguchan,' I heard my mother call. As I emerged from under the floors, I saw that the entire house was in smithereens. My mother, brother, and the neighbor emerged from the cloud of smoke with severe burns on their bodies.[2]

The buildings in Hiroshima were mainly wooden and the huge impact of the blast resulted in fires that ravaged the city. Many people died instantly, vaporized or killed by the fire. Others were blinded or suffered deep wounds from the effects of the explosions. The level of devastation was different from that witnessed through any previous type of bombing. There was no preparation for such an emergency, and the hospitals and treatment facilities were poorly prepared to care for the wounded.

Three days after Hiroshima, the US dropped another bomb, 'Fat Man', on the city of Nagasaki. This was an even bigger device, with a yield of 21 kilotons (equivalent to 21,000 tons of TNT).[3] Someone who lived through this later wrote:

> I was three years old at the time of the bombing. I don't remember much, but I do recall that my surroundings turned blindingly white, like a million camera flashes going off at once. ... Then, pitch darkness. Thankfully, I survived. But since that day, mysterious scabs began to form all over my body. I lost hearing in my left ear, probably due to the air blast. More than a decade after the bombing, my mother began to notice glass shards growing out of her skin – debris from the day of the bombing, presumably. My

> younger sister suffers from chronic muscle cramps to this day, on top of kidney issues that has her on dialysis three times a week.[4]

Many of those who were not initially killed by the blasts or inadequate medical treatment suffered from radiation poisoning. This included 'hair loss, bleeding gums, loss of energy, purple spots and high fevers'.[5] Scientific investigations have found that exposure to the fallout from the bombings has also led, in time, to cancer and heart failure.

Estimates of the death toll vary; the very nature of the blasts and a lack of wartime population figures has meant that it is impossible to ascertain the precise number killed in either city. Hiroshima had an estimated population of 255,260 at the time of the bombing and it is thought that 66,000 people were killed by the attack and 69,000 injured. Nagasaki had an estimated population of 195,250. When the bomb was dropped there on 9 August, 39,000 people were killed, many instantly, and 25,000 were injured.[6]

The Japanese government later established special medical provision for the *Hibakusha* (the people affected by the bomb), but their true numbers are hard to gauge. The bombings had a profound effect on Japanese society. The radiological contamination created by the bomb caused survivors to be stigmatized as different and as a result many were too ashamed to register to claim for care.

The US justified such horrific use of the bomb as necessary to defeat the Japanese emperor and end the war. Having caused horrendous devastation in Hiroshima, the decision to drop the second bomb in Nagasaki stemmed from a conviction held by US military leaders that nothing short of a catastrophic atomic attack would force the emperor to surrender. The US had entered the war four years earlier, in response to the Japanese bombing of Pearl Harbor. The war had ended in Europe in May 1945, but fighting continued in the Pacific with the US fighting the Japanese in Iwo Jima and Okinawa. In these conflicts the US had suffered an estimated 75,000 casualties.[7]

On 15 August 1945, a radio broadcast confirmed Japan's acceptance of the terms of the Potsdam Agreement. The official instrument of Japan's surrender was signed on 2 September 1945 by Foreign Minister Mamoru Shigemitsu and General Yoshijirō Umezu. The Second World War was over. The US had shown the world that it possessed a truly terrifying and world-changing weapon.

How aware were the US decision-makers of the effects of nuclear weapons in advance? They had witnessed the horrors of the war and feared the Nazis would develop atomic weapons. Did they know when they created the bomb that it would cause destruction on such a scale? Were they conscious that once these weapons had been developed, it was just a matter of time before other states acquired them?

I believe that the scientists and military planners behind the development of the atomic bomb and the decision to use it were aware that they were creating a massively powerful weapon and that it would cause a massive explosion. However, they were not aware of quite how significant this would be or of its long-term effects. Much like starting a fire, the spread and damage caused by the flames is not known until the fire has been lit.

These weapons have evolved over time into a *strategic deterrent*; in a changing geopolitical situation, states are deterred from conflict due to the fear that nuclear weapons will be used. This, however, is not the full story; these are also *political tools* of diplomacy and (in some cases) brinkmanship. Finally, the *moral dimension* of these weapons cannot be overlooked; the threat of nuclear war and the revulsion it triggers have led to international efforts to control these weapons, as well as public protest. This, in turn, has provoked enquiry into broader issues of environmental preservation, humanitarianism and social responsibility.

What are nuclear weapons?

Nuclear weapons are powerful explosive devices that use the energy released from nuclear reactions to cause destruction. The concept behind the nuclear bomb emerged from the successful splitting of the atom in 1938, a process known as nuclear fission.

Atomic bombs (fission bombs) are created by heavy atomic nuclei splitting into smaller parts. The splitting of the atoms causes huge amounts of energy to be released in the form of an explosion, shock wave or heat and radiation.

INTRODUCTION

> **Splitting the atom**
>
> The splitting of the atom is called fission. In this process, a neutron hits the nucleus of an atom of uranium or plutonium. Nuclear fusion is the process in which the two elements are joined together.
>
> This splitting process creates a huge amount of energy, which becomes 'self-sustaining', causing the chain reaction that produces an atomic explosion. The energy is then harnessed to create a nuclear weapon.

Nuclear bombs – also known as thermonuclear weapons (fusion bombs) – create an even more powerful reaction than atomic bombs. They rely on nuclear fusion, whereby light atomic nuclei, such as isotopes of hydrogen, are combined under extreme pressure and temperature to form a heavier nucleus.

Nuclear bombs often use an atomic bomb to trigger or initiate the fusion process. This creates weapons with much larger explosive power than atomic bombs. Enriched uranium and plutonium are needed to create any bomb.

Nuclear weapons work in three ways. First, they create an enormous explosion. Conventional weapons carry a yield (explosion power) measured in tons; nuclear weapons carry a yield a thousand times stronger, measured in kilotons. Some of the largest weapons developed are even measured in megatons. Second, the impact of the explosion and resulting fireball generates intense heat and pressure, creating a powerful updraft that pulls smoke and debris upward. As the hot gases rise and cool, they form the characteristic mushroom cloud associated with these weapons. Finally, fallout is released from the deadly explosion. This is highly toxic and covers a large radius around the blast site. The contamination is extensive in any area exposed to nuclear radiation, affecting animals and vegetation, thereby polluting the food chain.

It is extremely difficult to acquire nuclear weapons, since the process requires rare materials. One of the principal ingredients, enriched uranium, must be put through a complex process of purification, using advanced centrifuge equipment that is both complicated and expensive.

The design of nuclear weapons requires advanced scientific and engineering knowledge, as does the infrastructure to make them. Producing the materials for a nuclear weapon requires large and expensive facilities. Once developed, nuclear weapons can be launched from land, sea and air. It is not easy, however, to hide such a capability and to ensure success, any new weapon requires testing.

Paradoxically, while nuclear knowledge can be used to produce deadly weapons of war, it can also be adapted to create huge scientific advances in medicine, the environment and as an alternative source of energy. For this reason, harnessing nuclear knowledge for nuclear energy and technology has been globally desirable and has been seen as a badge of honour.

Japan, Germany and South Korea, for example, all have advanced nuclear power facilities.

> **The nuclear powers**
>
> Only a handful of states have nuclear weapons, and most of them like the world to know they have them, as they provide power and prestige. Out of 195 sovereign states in the world, nine have nuclear weapons, including the US, UK, Russia, China and France. These states also sit as the permanent members of the United Nations (UN) Security Council and have the power to veto decisions. India, Pakistan, North Korea and Israel also have nuclear weapons, although Israel has never declared its capability.

Power in the Cold War

Nuclear weapons are inevitably associated with the Cold War and, in order to understand their significance today, we need to look back at their history. In 1949, the Soviet Union was the second state to develop its own nuclear capability, and in the decades that followed, the UK (1952), France (1960) and China (1964) followed suit. In the growing arms race from 1949 to 1990 between the US and Soviet Union, each side competed to build bigger, more powerful weapons. To many, nuclear weapons kept the Cold War cold, but the arms race created an uneasy balance of power. The development of thermonuclear weapons by both the US (1952) and Soviet Union (1953) only intensified the nuclear threat; these weapons were about 700 times more powerful than the atomic bombs used in Hiroshima and Nagasaki. Fusion technology means they can be more compact and deadly, capable of generating far greater explosive yields than their predecessors.

During the Cold War, the Soviet Union largely focused its military planning on building bigger warheads capable of causing more and more destruction. At its height, the Soviet Union developed a bomb named 'Tsar Bomb' with a yield of 50 megatons, believed to be the biggest nuclear weapon ever successfully test-fired. The US varied its capability, also developing smaller, more adaptable weapons. The MIRV (Multiple Independently Targetable Re-entry Vehicle) weapon, for example, is a ballistic weapon containing multiple warheads. On detonation, it can release several smaller-yield warheads that fire in multiple directions. While it would not cause the same mass destructive effect as a single high-yield bomb, a weapon of this kind could still provide a massive strategic advantage. The US also developed tactical nuclear weapons: smaller, lower-yield weapons that were easier to transport, travelled a shorter distance, generated less fallout and were stationed within North Atlantic Treaty Organization (NATO) member states throughout Europe.

INTRODUCTION

Nuclear weapons today

The nuclear threat still remains today. Social and technological advances have changed the nature of warfare, to the extent that now the threats we face transcend individual states and affect the very tools from which we build our societies, endangering our personal communication, banking, the power grid and air traffic control systems needed for everyday travel. Cybersecurity and the threat of a cyber-attack dominate strategic thinking, coupled with advances in artificial intelligence and robotic warfare. Drone technology has advanced massively within the last ten years. Drones can be used to courier information and survey large areas. They can also be used for targeted killings and on the battlefield in wartime. The conflict in Ukraine has demonstrated this; both Russia and Ukraine have used drones throughout the war.

As the nature of warfare has changed, so too has nuclear weapons development. The modernization of nuclear weapons has led to the development of smaller, more adaptable weapons. Low-yield nuclear weapons can now be loaded onto short-range missiles and used on the battlefield. It is believed that the smallest tactical nuclear weapon to have been developed was the Davy Crockett US system, which was as small as 10–20 tons (0.01–0.02 kilotons).[8] (The bomb dropped on Hiroshima was 15 kilotons.)

Technological innovations in war have brought us a new third nuclear age. This is an era in which we are also seeing advanced developments in conventional weapons. The academics Fabian Hoffmann and

William Alberque have drawn a distinction between kinetic and non-kinetic weapons.[9] Kinetic weapons use the ability to cause damage through the energy of their impact; examples include cruise missiles, hypersonic weapons and unmanned aerial vehicles (drones). Non-kinetic weapons are those which affect the electromagnetic environment, leaving no direct impact in the sense of a collision, but still cause significant disruption, such as cyber-attacks and electronic methods of warfare. All of these weapons have the potential to cause mass destruction. They may alter the strategic options of states in a crisis and can have the potential to change the outcome of war, rivalling nuclear weapons.[10] Yet, despite this, nuclear weapons still dominate the headlines and political decision-making.

Strategic power alone does not explain why nuclear weapons stand out from other weapons of war. If this was their only value, we would, in eight decades, have likely seen nuclear weapons used more than twice.

Politics and diplomacy: deterrence

Nuclear weapons are also unique tools for political diplomacy and bargaining. Traditionally, it has been widely believed that the threat of the use of nuclear weapons deters any would-be aggressor from attacking a nuclear state out of fear of the consequences. This is the fundamental principle behind the strategy of deterrence, which rests on the perception that nuclear weapons could and may be used. This has been the basis for a lot of the posturing and rhetoric of states since 1945. Russia's statements throughout the war in Ukraine are just one example of this. Great care has been taken by nuclear weapon states to remind their potential enemies of the deadly military advantage they have, while also taking care not to push so hard that they may find themselves in a position where they have *no option* but to use their weapons. So far, the international community has been willing to coexist with this balance.

The US strategist Bernard Brodie declared in 1945, after the Hiroshima and Nagasaki bombings, that the sheer power generated by a nuclear explosion would change the very nature of warfare. Such terrible weapons meant that the costs of any conflict to human life would outweigh any perceived advantage; the advantage of nuclear weapons was that they would deter states from seeking conflict.

Political and diplomatic pressure has also led states to give up their nuclear programmes. During the 1990s, after the Cold War, South Africa and Ukraine signed international agreements relinquishing their nuclear development facilities. In the case of Ukraine, which had the world's third largest nuclear arsenal on its territory, warheads were transferred to Russia for elimination.

The use and proliferation of nuclear weapons is also banned by international law. In 1970, the Treaty on the Non-Proliferation of Nuclear Weapons (NPT) entered into force and 43 states signed it. The NPT limits the possession of nuclear weapons to a handful of states who had declared their nuclear capability prior to 1967. The treaty has near universal membership. As of 2025, 191 states have acceded to the treaty. The NPT addresses both vertical and horizontal proliferation. The former refers to the expansion, improvement and development of nuclear weapons by states that have already acquired nuclear technology, and the latter refers to an increase in the number of states with nuclear weapons. While the treaty does not ban the development of nuclear weapons, it does seek to limit proliferation. Nuclear states keep their nuclear weapons but agree not to help other states develop nuclear weapons or to transfer nuclear technology. They pledge to work towards disarmament. Non-nuclear states agree not to develop nuclear weapons and, in exchange, receive access to the benefits of nuclear energy, and the nuclear science and technology associated with it.

Despite the progress of the NPT, the strategic advantage that nuclear weapons enable has still been a lure for states. Israel, India and Pakistan remain outside of the treaty and have developed nuclear weapons. Israel has never declared its nuclear capability, but is thought to have developed its programme by 1967. It has adopted a policy of nuclear ambiguity, neither confirming nor denying this. India acquired nuclear weapons in 1998 and Pakistan in 1998. North Korea, having been a member of the NPT, withdrew its membership in January 2003 and successfully test-fired a nuclear weapon in 2006. Iran's nuclear programme continues to be of international concern.

Norms and morality: the symbolic distinction of nuclear weapons

Finally, alongside the strategic power and political qualities of nuclear weapons is the symbolic value and the potential status of elitism and prestige that nuclear weapons confer. Nuclear weapons act as an extension of the cultural identity of the state. Motivations for states to acquire nuclear weapons have been shaped by national pride, religion, history and the geographical vulnerability of the state. These factors fuel the strategic value of these weapons and explain why some states try to develop nuclear weapons, despite intense international risk and pressure, and others do not. Acquiring such a capability puts states in an exclusive club.

Global awareness of the power and destruction of these weapons, in addition to the long-term devastating pollution that their use creates, presents a moral paradox. Should the declared nuclear states choose to use their weapons, they would almost certainly lose this status and prestige. For the other four states, India, Pakistan, North Korea and Israel, any such use would lead to exclusion and condemnation from the international community. This would also, in many cases, go against the cultural identity of these states. So far, for all, the symbolism of power and status has outweighed any military, strategic calculations that might favour use. The defensive property of nuclear weapons and the political bargaining that such capability has facilitated have been too great. Both India and China have in the past issued no first use policies, stating that nuclear weapons will only be used as a weapon of last resort in the event of an attack. Nuclear weapons, they say, are purely defensive.

Academics and politicians have argued that, in fact, a *taboo* has emerged towards the use of nuclear weapons, derived from the strategic and moral concerns about the consequences of their use. The taboo is largely a result of long-standing public antipathy towards nuclear weapons. Democratic states have been influenced by grassroots movements campaigning for nuclear abolition. The taboo formed around an understanding that certain global standards (norms) set the framework for international behaviour. The use of nuclear weapons is seen as a morally distinct and repugnant practice.

The following chapters address all of the themes discussed and provide a mostly chronological account of how nuclear weapons have developed through time.

Do nuclear weapons make the world safer? US presidents Kennedy and Reagan, as well as the US economist and strategist Thomas Schelling, all argued that they have secured global peace *because* their deadly potential prevented their use. The counter-argument to this is that we have had many (non-nuclear) conflicts since 1945 which nuclear weapons have failed to prevent.

Proponents of nuclear abolition point to the horrific effects of nuclear weapons and the dangers of nuclear accidents and use. They urge the world to give up nuclear weapons, yet this is easier said than done, once the knowledge to produce them is available.

INTRODUCTION

In the next chapters, I examine the role nuclear weapons have played in geopolitics over the last eight decades. What risks have they brought and how have they been understood both by leaders and populations? I unpick the changes in strategy, acquisition, non-proliferation and public attitudes to try to determine the role of nuclear weapons today and in the future.

Ultimately, nuclear weapons serve as a reminder of the barbarism of war but also of the importance of the preservation of humanity and peace.

2
ORIGINS

To appreciate the purpose of nuclear weapons, we need to explore the circumstances in which they were developed and used. In this chapter and the next, I shall focus on their strategic significance and power through this lens. I explore the origins of the US Manhattan Project, which developed the atomic bomb, fearing that Hitler would do this first and thereby create a Nazi ultimate weapon. If he had succeeded, it would have put total victory within his grasp. The project was a collaborative effort by UK, US, Canadian and German expatriate scientists to achieve mastery of the nuclear field before Hitler. Many of the scientists behind the project came to have serious misgivings about the bomb being used.

Despite this, as touched on in the opening chapter, nuclear weapons were used in August 1945 on the Japanese cities of Hiroshima and Nagasaki. Here I want to explore the consequences of this, examining the extent to which US policy makers truly knew the effects of the bomb.

The chapter concludes by examining the broader global strategic and political significance of the use of the bomb in the post-war world. Hostility and secrecy dominated relations between the Allied powers. Among US senators there was a desire to maintain and strengthen the strategic advantage they had acquired by using the bomb. US political and military leaders chose to cease working with the UK, abandoning the Manhattan Project and running their own nuclear weapons programme. They rightly feared that it was only a matter of time before other states also acquired these weapons. In 1949, the Soviet Union tested its own atomic bomb, changing the nuclear dynamic and triggering the arms race.

The historical significance of breakthroughs in military science and technology provide insight into why atomic weapons became strategically important. Technological innovations such as the invention of the tank, long-range artillery, machine guns and chemical weapons around the turn of the 20th century highlighted the increasingly deadly nature of warfare. The use of these weapons in the First World War made this abundantly clear.

During the inter-war period, under the auspices of the League of Nations, international heads of state sought to regulate weapons that caused 'unnecessary' suffering. These efforts built on the Hague Conventions from before the First World War, which had tried to rein in the increasing destructiveness of war by banning certain weapons. This was the basis of the later Geneva Protocol (1925), which prohibited chemical and biological weapons. These efforts ultimately failed. While there was relatively little use of chemical weapons in the Second World War, as will be discussed in later chapters, the development of airpower and the strategy of aerial bombing proved that warfare had become total, reaching both civilians and combatants. The German bombing campaign on the UK during the Blitz, for example, killed an estimated 40,000 people over a period of seven months, from September 1940 to May 1941. In total, the UK civilian death toll in the war is estimated to be 70,000 people, significantly higher than 2,000 in the First World War.[1] The Allied powers' firebombing campaign on the German city of Hamburg in the last week of July 1943 killed an estimated 34,000 to 43,000 people and the bombing of Dresden in February 1945 25,000.[2]

Scientific developments at this time included advances in rocketry, jet propulsion, and research into more powerful and destructive explosives. But it was the knowledge of how to split the atom that provided the greatest breakthrough of all.

On 17 December 1938, German scientists Otto Hahn and Fritz Strassmann submitted the manuscript detailing how they had discovered how to split uranium atoms into smaller elements. It was published in January 1939.[3] This research was ground-breaking, but Hahn and Strassmann were not the only nuclear physicists working to find ways to harness nuclear energy. The field of scientists in this domain was small, with many working closely with Fritz and Strassmann in Europe or the Soviet Union. Those in Europe had seen first-hand the power of the Nazi party, having witnessed Nazi rule, and realized the dangers of Hitler acquiring an atomic bomb.

In August of the following year, on the eve of the Second World War, the Hungarian-American physicist Leo Szilard and his German-American colleague, Albert Einstein, wrote to President Roosevelt to warn him that 'the element uranium may be turned into a new and important source of energy'. Szilard and Einstein implored Roosevelt to act to change this, arguing that there was now the possibility that 'extremely powerful bombs of a new type may be constructed'.[4] Today, uranium supplies are sourced from many parts of the world, but at the time of Szilard and Einstein's letter, it was thought that there were very limited supplies of uranium, concentrated in Czechoslovakia, the Belgian Congo and Canada. Hitler had occupied Czechoslovakia, thereby controlling that supply of uranium. Both men were concerned that this would bring Germany a step closer to developing a deadly bomb. They proposed that the US should develop a programme to monitor scientific development and start working on a similar weapons programme. Roosevelt responded by establishing the Advisory Committee on Uranium.

A month later, German forces invaded Poland and the war began. Over the coming years, the German project to develop a bomb would move into full development. German scientists masked their research, claiming they were working on a uranium reactor project that could be used to develop submarine engines.[5]

The Manhattan Project

The UK was also working on its own atomic energy programme, but weakened by the war, the only way it could pursue its research was through collaboration. In July 1940, despite earlier reservations, the UK informally offered to give the US access to its scientific research. In part this decision was driven by a desire to encourage the US to join the war; it was also due to a lack of resources and staff to fully capitalize on its scientific progress. British scientists discovered that the US project was not as advanced as their own research.

Despite sharing scientific knowledge, neither the UK nor US were eager to collaborate. But as the war wore on, the UK became more stretched financially and in terms of personnel. Germany had attacked UK cities and industrial bases in its Blitzkrieg bombing campaigns and had occupied much of Europe. In 1941 Japan entered the war, having formed an alliance with Germany and Italy in September 1940, and at the end of that year, the US joined the conflict too.

A year later, US intelligence identified that Hitler was building a new deadly weapon at a fast pace; Allied forces received evidence that German scientists had manufactured the V-1 flying bomb, the V-2 rocket, Tiger Tanks, the ME262 jet fighter and the MP44 assault rifle, which increased concern about Hitler's ambition for an atomic bomb.

The US and UK finally recognized in June 1942 that they could achieve more by working together. Both sides believed that the development of an atomic bomb would give them the strategic advantage that they needed to defeat Germany. They pooled resources and scientific knowledge to establish the Manhattan Project. In 1943, Canada signed the Quebec Agreement, joining the Manhattan Project. (The French government, and French scientists, were involved in the early stages of the project but France was not an official partner on the project.) Many of the nuclear physicists working on the project had emigrated to the US and the UK, fleeing persecution under the Nazis. It was a massive undertaking: at its peak it employed 130,000 people and cost an estimated US$2.2 billion at the time.[6] It was essential that the project remained secret; not even the US vice president or Congress were aware of it.

While the project was under way, US intelligence was investigating the extent of the German atomic programme. The Alsos Mission,[7] a secret intelligence mission administered by the US army intelligence unit led by General Leslie Groves, was sent on three assignments to Italy, Paris and Germany to recover documents and equipment and interrogate German scientists in exile and their relatives. They discovered that the German atomic programme had not advanced to the extent they had imagined. Nonetheless, the Manhattan Project went on.

On 16 July 1945, the scientists' hard work came to fruition with the test-firing of an atomic bomb at

White Sands missile range, New Mexico. It proved their theories correct: a successful atomic bomb had been created. This success gave the Allies unmatched strategic power. They knew that they had developed a deadly weapon, but did not know the full extent of its power. Was it enough to possess this weapon, or did they need to use it? Did those creating the bomb really know it had the potential to cause all-out devastation? The answer to both questions is complex. The scientists working on the bomb were certainly aware of the significance of this discovery and therefore scared that this could get into the hands of the Nazi regime. The military and politicians on the project understood the strategic advantage that this weapon gave them, but may not have known its full effects. As Kimball describes, 'a number of military "experts" tended to see the bomb as nothing more than just a bigger bang. Churchill also underestimated the weapon. … After all this new bomb is just going to be bigger than our present bombs and it involves no difference in the principles of war'.[8]

After six years of war, German defeat on its Eastern front, the liberation of Europe and the death of Hitler, the war in Europe finally came to an end with the declaration of Victory in Europe (VE) Day on 8 May 1945. But Japan remained at war; having occupied much of Asia, from Hong Kong to Burma, it advanced its dominance within the region and still presented a substantial threat to the US. The US was sustaining significant losses in this theatre, and faced a prolonged war and many more casualties.

ORIGINS

Five months prior to the White Sands missile tests, in early February 1945, the Allied powers, the UK, US and Soviet Union, met in Yalta, Crimea, to discuss the future of Europe. Roosevelt wanted the Soviet Union to be part of a newly formed UN and also sought Soviet support for the war in the Pacific against Japan. Churchill called for free and fair democratic elections in Europe. But Stalin posed a new threat to Europe: he wanted Soviet control of Poland and to develop a sphere of influence as a buffer between the Soviet Union and the Western world. The architects of the Manhattan Project sought not only a solution to end the war in the Pacific, but also a way to demonstrate their strategic superiority, and believed the bomb was the means to this end.

Politically, the success of the Manhattan Project gave the UK and the US confidence to negotiate with Stalin over the reconstruction of Europe. Stalin knew about the Manhattan Project though he had not been formally told about it. Truman felt that the development of the bomb provided a tool of leverage and a massive strategic advantage.

Four days before the use of the bomb, the Allied powers met again, this time in a defeated Germany, at Potsdam, to continue their discussion of Europe's future. The preceding months had seen momentous political change in both the US and the UK. Franklin Roosevelt died on 12 April 1945 and was succeeded by Harry S. Truman as 33rd president of the US. Winston Churchill had lost the UK government elections on 5 July to the Labour Party under Clement Attlee.

The discussions at Potsdam addressed the annexation of Germany and the Soviet and US war with Japan. For Truman, the breakthrough of the atom bomb provided an advantage over Stalin. He mentioned to the Soviet leader that the US 'planned to drop the most powerful explosive ever made on the Japanese',[9] a clear indicator that he realized the strategic significance of the bomb, even if not yet its longer-term impact.

Despite this rhetoric, Truman himself was saddened by the consequences of the war, having visited Berlin on his way to Potsdam. He saw the destruction of the city and wrote in his diary on 16 July 1945 in Potsdam, 'I hope for some sort of peace, but I fear that machines are ahead of morals by centuries and when morals catch up perhaps there'll be no reason for any of it'. He added: 'I hope not. But we are only termites on a planet and maybe when we bore too deeply into the planet there'll be a reckoning. Who knows?'[10]

With the war in Europe now over, many of the scientists on the Manhattan Project called for the bomb not to be used and argued that the mere capability to *produce* the bomb was enough to ensure security. They sent the so-called Szilard petition to President Truman on 17 July 1945, signed by 67 of the project scientists. It reasoned against the use of the bomb as this would open the door to a deadly new future: 'Atomic bombs are primarily the means for the ruthless annihilation of cities. Once they were introduced as an instrument of war it would be difficult to resist for long the temptation of putting them to such use.'[11]

The scientists were not alone in these concerns. The US Secretary for War Henry Stimson, though taking a tough stance towards Japan, had written to President Truman a day earlier, on 2 July 1945, stating that 'there is reason to believe that the operation for the occupation of Japan following the landing may be a very long, costly and arduous struggle on our part'. The Soviet Union had joined the war in China and the Japanese were vastly outnumbered by the Americans. Stimson recommended that the US warn Japan to surrender. He noted that:

> Japan *is* susceptible to reason in such a crisis to a much greater extent than is indicated by our current press and other current comment. Japan is not a nation composed wholly of mad fanatics of an entirely different mentality from ours. On the contrary, she has within the past century shown herself to possess extremely intelligent people, capable in an unprecedentedly short time of adopting not only the complicated technique of Occidental civilization but to a substantial extent their culture and their political and social ideas. Her advance in all these respects during the short period of sixty or seventy years has been one of the most astounding feats of national progress in history. (emphasis in original)[12]

Truman adopted Stimson's recommendation. The Potsdam declaration read that Japan faced 'prompt and utter destruction' if it did not surrender.[13] The Japanese military ignored this threat.

Hiroshima and after

On 25 July 1945, the order was given to drop the atomic bomb on the city of Hiroshima. The data of population density in both cities in the months prior to the use of the bombs differs greatly, as there was no definitive source. Based on rice rationing figures, it estimated that the population at the time within Hiroshima was 255,260, with Nagasaki estimated to have a population of 195,250.[14]

When considering how aware military planners were of the full consequences of the use of the bomb it is important to consider why the cities of Hiroshima and Nagasaki were chosen. The planning committee in charge of both operations had a long list of potential sites to target and chose three criteria: any target needed to be large, to have high strategic value and needed not to have been part of the US firebombing campaign which began in March 1945.[15]

Hiroshima had remained relatively unscathed by bombing raids during the war, as the US maintained its strategic focus on other cities with greater strategic and industrial significance, such as Tokyo and Nagoya. These cities were seen as more critical to Japan's war effort. Despite this, Hiroshima was a major port and military headquarters and thus, to the planners, a strategic target.[16]

Nagasaki was not originally on the list of locations for the atomic bomb. Kyoto had been the next target city. It too had not been bombed and contained major factories. There were also many historical sites there and it was home to almost 2,000 Buddhist temples and

Shinto shrines.[17] Scientists on the panel thought that the people of Kyoto would be more affected by the use of the bomb as the city was home to several universities, prompting the assumption that 'the people of Kyoto would be more apt to appreciate the significance of such a weapon as the gadget'.[18] (Use of such a term as 'the gadget' indicates the disassociation by some members of the panel from the magnitude of the effects of the bomb.) Ultimately, the planners decided against Kyoto due to its cultural significance. Secretary of War Henry Stimson had visited the city many times and had even honeymooned there. Instead, they chose Nagasaki, a port city located between two mountains, with a thriving shipbuilding industry.

After the use of the first bomb in Hiroshima, the White House released a statement to the American people, stressing the new strategic advantage that the bomb had bestowed:

> With this bomb we have added a new and revolutionary increase in destruction to supplement the growing power of our armed forces. ... The fact that we can release atomic energy ushers in a new era in Man's understanding of nature's forces. Atomic energy may in the future supplement coal, oil and falling water, but at present it cannot be produced on a basis to compete with them commercially. Until that comes there must be a long period of intensive research.[19]

This statement highlighted the physical power of the bomb, but did not recognize the wider devastation that this caused, or the long-term political and strategic impact of this. This would only be understood in time.

Two days after the second atomic bomb was dropped on Nagasaki, the US military organized a special Manhattan Project Atomic Bomb Investigating Group to assess the impact on both cities. The aim was to secure and uncover all information regarding the effects of the bombs, and radioactive impact or unusual hazards. This found that:

> The central portions of the cities under the explosions suffered almost complete destruction. Casualties in such buildings near the centre of the explosion were almost 100%. Fires spread up all over the wide flat central area of the city: These fires soon combined into an immense firestorm. Everything was destroyed within a mile of the centre of the explosion.[20]

In August 1945, Stalin declared war on Japan, claiming this was in fulfilment of a promise to join the war after the defeat of Germany. By joining with the Allies, Stalin was strengthening the Allied position in the wake of the use of the bomb. These factors forced Japan to sign the official instrument of surrender on 2 September 1945. The war was over.

To the majority of the US public, the true consequences of the bombings were unknown. When they were made aware of the images and death toll from both bombings, initially these were lost to the strategic victory that it had delivered. The war was over and to many this was because of the US atomic bombing campaign. Opinion polls in August 1945 indicated that the atomic bomb was seen as just another weapon amid the horrors of the war: a means to an end. A Gallup poll from August 1945 found that 85 per cent of Americans supported its use, 10 per cent opposed it and 5 per cent were uncertain.[21] Media coverage was controlled by government censorship and initially downplayed the impact. Most accounts justified the bombings and 'portrayed the cities and their inhabitants as symbolising the rebirth of a new, peace-minded Japan'.[22]

One of the first sources to counter this narrative came from journalist John Hersey's article, 'Hiroshima', in the August 1946 *New Yorker*. An editorial introduction read:

> The *New Yorker* this week devotes its entire editorial space to an article on the almost complete obliteration of a city by one atomic bomb, and what happened to the people of that city. It does so in the conviction that few of us have yet comprehended the all but incredible destructive power of this weapon, and that everyone might well take time to consider the terrible implications of its use.[23]

Hersey described the experiences of six Hiroshima survivors, and in doing so provided the first detailed media coverage of the reality and human costs of atomic war.

As awareness grew about the impact of the bomb, many leading military and political strategists who had worked on the Manhattan Project, or were associated with US policy at this time, expressed their regret and concerns about this in their memoirs. General Douglas MacArthur, Supreme Commander for the Allied powers during the war, allegedly confided that he was 'appalled and depressed by this Frankenstein monster'.[24] Admiral Halsey, Commander of the US Third Fleet, testified before Congress in September 1949 that 'the atomic bombing of civilians is morally indefensible'.[25] Yet despite their recognition of its horrific effects, these planners were unwilling to give up the bomb or to share this knowledge.

Shortly after the atomic bombings, US government officials chose to go it alone, and removed the UK from involvement in their future nuclear programme. At least 30 British scientists had worked with the US on the Manhattan Project. Despite this, the US felt that sharing nuclear knowledge was far too dangerous for the world. Democratic Senator and Presiding Officer of the US Senate Kenneth McKellar expressed the view that: 'It seems unwise, impolitic and dangerous to our nation's defence, provocative of war, and dangerous to peace to give the formula to Russia, England, Canada or any other nation.'[26] If the knowledge of how to produce the bomb were shared with the UK, it would need to be shared with other nations.

The decision was also strategic. The US did not yet fully know the value of the atomic bomb and so was reluctant to share this knowledge with others until it did. McKellar was concerned that 'to give the formula for this weapon to other nations or to any other nation without money and without price would be to invite them to get busy and prepare for another world war'.[27]

Yet despite the wish to maintain a strategic advantage, US decision-makers feared the future proliferation of the bomb. They recognized that, in time, others were very likely to also acquire this capability. During the early Cold War period, debates in Congress shifted to how to safeguard nuclear knowledge. Democrat Senator Robert F. Wagner from New York, Republican Senator William Langer of North Dakota and Democrat Senator for Florida Claude Pepper all called for nuclear information to be shared with Stalin, so that all Allies had this knowledge. Despite this, the majority of Congressmen opposed this. Most vocal were McKellar and Senator Arthur H. Vandenberg, a Republican from Michigan; both believed that sharing the secrets of the atomic bomb would endanger US security. More widely, it was felt that the nuclear genie was now out of the bottle and no one had any clear plan as to how it could be contained.

The scientists behind the Manhattan Project did not trust the Soviet Union. Many had escaped the Soviet Union during the war and had read about Stalin's Great Purge show trials of the late 1930s. Before the use of the bomb, in June 1945, they produced the Franck report, which warned that it would be only a matter of three to five years before the Soviet Union acquired its own atomic capability. It was not possible to avoid an arms race, they suggested, either by 'keeping secret from the competing nations the basic scientific facts of nuclear power, or by cornering the raw materials required for such a race'.[28] In March 1946, Churchill gave his famous 'Iron Curtain' speech in which he warned:

> [F]rom Stettin in the Baltic to Trieste in the Adriatic, an iron curtain has descended across the continent. Behind that line lie all of the capitals of the ancient states of central and eastern Europe. Warsaw, Berlin, Prague, Vienna, Budapest, Belgrade, Bucharest and Sofia, all these famous cities and populations around them lie in what I must call the Soviet sphere, and all are subject in one form or another, not only to Soviet influence but to a very high and in some cases increasing measure of control from Moscow.[29]

Referring to Stalin, Churchill said, 'from what I have seen of our Russian friends and Allies during the war, I am convinced that there is nothing they admire so much as strength and there is nothing for which they have less respect than for military weakness'.[30] Should Stalin have the capability, Churchill had no doubt he would certainly develop a Soviet Union atomic bomb.

The first incident in which the US used its strategic advantage against the Soviet Union was the Berlin blockade, which lasted from 24 June 1948 to 12 May 1949. Berlin was divided after the war into four zones, with the UK, US, France and the Soviet Union each having responsibility for one of them. The city lay 100 miles inside Soviet-controlled East Germany and the blockade was an attempt by the Soviet Union to gain complete control of Berlin by cutting off access to it, trapping and forcing Allied powers to withdraw.

In response, Western forces airlifted in food and other supplies. During the blockade, Truman ordered three bomber groups of B-29 Superfortress aeroplanes to be stationed in the UK. Strategically, this decision was seen as an extension of US nuclear forces. The US, still the sole nuclear power, used this advantage to deter Stalin from further expansion into Europe. The blockade lasted almost a year until Stalin, citing economic pressures, lifted it.

Concerns about the Soviet Union's nuclear ambitions were justified. In 1949, the Soviet Union declared it had successfully tested a nuclear weapon. Since 1939, Soviet scientists, like their US and UK counterparts, had been working on harnessing the atom. They too feared a Nazi atomic bomb. The Soviet programme received very little funding, Stalin instead focused on implementing the five-year plan and maintaining the Soviet war effort.

It was only in 1945, after the US had used the bomb, that work on the Soviet nuclear project came into full force. As the war was ending, Soviet troops entered annexed Germany and launched 'trophy brigades', which requisitioned any possessions or information that they could find relating to the German atomic project. Many people had fled Germany by this time, but any remaining scientists were rounded up and sent to the Soviet Union. In addition, the Soviets seized enriched uranium, which they were short of, to develop their programme.

The Soviet Union also gained nuclear information through intelligence and espionage. The KGB obtained thousands of pages of technical information about the Manhattan Project from German scientists, who were believed to be sympathetic to communism. Manhattan Project scientists and project workers Klaus Fuchs, Bruno Pontecorvo, Alan Nunn May and David Greenglass, as well as Julius and Ethel Rosenberg who were executed for spying, all shared nuclear information with the Soviet Union.

Nuclear weapons were clearly here to stay. The Soviet nuclear programme was about to change the global order. Where would this lead?

3
THE COLD WAR

By 1949, two states had nuclear weapons. Did that mean the world was getting safer or more dangerous? What were nuclear weapons for now that the world was on the brink of an arms race?

Developments in military technology did not stop with the atomic bomb; nuclear physicists continued to explore the possibilities that splitting the atom presented. In 1952, US scientists successfully produced nuclear fusion, which resulted in the production of thermonuclear weapons. A year later, the Soviet Union also developed this technology; the world was looking more and more dangerous.

This growing threat contributed to the strategy of deterrence. In 1945, the US military strategist Bernard Brodie recognized that no military planning could counter the destructiveness of nuclear weapons. 'Thus far our chief purpose has been to win wars. From now on its chief purpose must be to avert them. It can have almost no other useful purpose.'[1] Instead, the US needed to consider ways in which war could be prevented. Describing nuclear weapons as 'the absolute weapon', he advocated that future policy should concentrate on preventing their use. Over time, as political differences between the US and Soviet Union increased, this policy morphed into a strategy known as Mutually Assured Destruction (MAD). Central to MAD was the calculation that both nuclear powers had enough warheads to create complete annihilation. The concept relied upon the ability of the US to respond to any threat from the Soviet Union with overwhelming counter-force to ensure absolute destruction. Central to this was the ability of the US to have a second-strike capability, which meant it could respond to any potential attack with weapons launched by sea, air and land and from multiple locations. The increased production of nuclear weapons was essential to ensure this.

Throughout the 1950s and 1960s the strategic appeal of nuclear weapons proved too great for other powers: the UK, France and China acquired their own nuclear capability. These three states were also members of the UN Security Council (China became a permanent member of the UN Security Council in 1971) and had the power to veto United Nations amendments. Acquiring nuclear weapons enabled them to have even greater political power as this was backed up by strategic might, thus elevating these states into an elite club of nuclear powers with heightened status and prestige.

The technological challenges and costs of developing a nuclear weapons programme have always been huge obstacles to proliferation, but many states without the ability to produce nuclear weapons of their own still wanted the strategic protection they provided. Recognition of this led, in 1949, to the establishment of NATO. NATO highlights the growing reliance on nuclear weapons as a guarantee of security, but also the growing desire to increase international cooperation to deter Soviet expansionism. NATO was established as a collective security organization made up of Canada, the US and Western European states; this provided a nuclear security umbrella, whereby 'an attack on one is an attack on all'. Under the terms of the founding treaty, nuclear weapon states guaranteed the security of non-nuclear states in Western Europe, with the aim of preventing Soviet expansion and ensuring the safety of member states. To counter the presence of NATO, the Soviet Union created the Warsaw Pact in 1955, which provided a nuclear security umbrella for all of the Soviet satellites in Central and Eastern Europe.

Initially, after the successful Soviet test in 1949, the US hoped that nuclear war could be contained through diplomatic means. US intelligence identified that the Soviet acquisition of the bomb did not necessarily increase the danger of war; the Soviets wished to match their military power with that of the US, but did not seek another war. US policy was to foster the UN as a way to control the threat from the Soviet Union. Their belief was that by promoting democracy, war could be averted.

WHAT ARE NUCLEAR WEAPONS FOR?

In 1949, US policy makers created a question-and-answer factsheet about the perceived Soviet threat. This was summarized in a confidential telegram sent to all US embassies and consulates, making the case that war with the Soviet Union was not inevitable:

> Everyone knows the preparation for aggressive war is impossible in a democracy and even more so in a coalition of democracies. If there is danger of war it stems from the attitudes and policies of others. We have no means of knowing what is in the minds of men who control the government of the Soviet Union. We should remember that the mere fact that a country might have the ability to make a bomb would not in itself be an assurance to that country of overall military superiority. The belief of this government is that war is not inevitable; and our policies continue to be directed to this avoidance (Question 11).[2]

The memo identified that, as it was inevitable that other states would want to acquire nuclear weapons, the only way to discourage this was through the promotion of international norms of democracy and peace: 'We must never forget that the atomic weapon, terrible as it is, is only one element in the complex pattern of political and military realities, which determines the security of this country.'[3]

Interestingly, at this time, US political and military planners were beginning to acknowledge the nuclear paradox: while nuclear weapons guaranteed strategic strength, the moral opprobrium associated with the bomb acted as a stimulus to seek alternative measures to maintain peace. US national government policy planners noted that: 'We will wait to see whether the consciousness of possessing this terrible and destructive weapon will bring to the Soviet leaders something of that same sense of responsibility to the peoples of the world.'[4]

Despite hopes for increased diplomacy, the political differences between the Soviet Union and the West were increasing. Communist North Korea's invasion of South Korea in 1950, US intervention and the ensuing war seemed to justify Western anxiety about the expansion of communism. China was also seen as a growing strategic threat. American strategists believed that North Korea was propped up by China and China was acting for the Soviet Union, 'under direct orders from Moscow'.[5] The Korean War gave greater prominence to strategic arguments that the US needed to increase its nuclear capability to counter communist expansionism. China's role in the war demonstrated the spread of the communist influence throughout Asia. Western leaders predicted that without strategic power, this expansion could not be prevented.

US policy involved expanding its nuclear arsenal and reinforcing the strategy of MAD. It focused upon a massive rearmament programme and on heightening the development of its nuclear capability. Nuclear weapons were now a strategic priority and the cornerstone of any arms development or planning. In the US, jobs and security now depended on this new invention; from 1950 to 1953, defence spending almost tripled, from 8.09 per cent to 14.2 per cent of gross domestic product.[6] It reduced to 10 per cent after the war, and stayed roughly at this figure throughout the Cold War.[7] The academic Anne Harrington de Santana has written that advanced nuclear weapons represented the ultimate embodiment of power – they have become fetish objects of force. 'The combination of nuclear explosive technology with advanced missile systems maximised the capacity for physical destruction, while minimizing the human presence necessary to engage in the act of destruction.'[8]

Scientific innovation had led to the development of thermonuclear weapons, indicating that the deadly potential of war was only likely to increase. The US under the Eisenhower administration adopted a strategic posture of massive retaliation (1953). This strategy embodied the principles of MAD and set out how the US would respond in the event of a nuclear attack. In such an event, the US needed to show that it could absorb a nuclear strike and retaliate with a second strike of nuclear weapons. It was essential to communicate that it had the capability to cause devastating destruction and the will to do so. Developing a massive arms manufacturing programme was one way of conveying this.

The need to deter the Soviet Union meant that the US had to ensure strategic stability, whereby it communicated that it had enough weapons to threaten and deter the Soviet Union against an attack, but not enough to cause Soviet powers to pre-empt an attack and strike first. Each side needed to acquire and maintain enough offensive and defensive weapons to achieve this balance.

THE COLD WAR

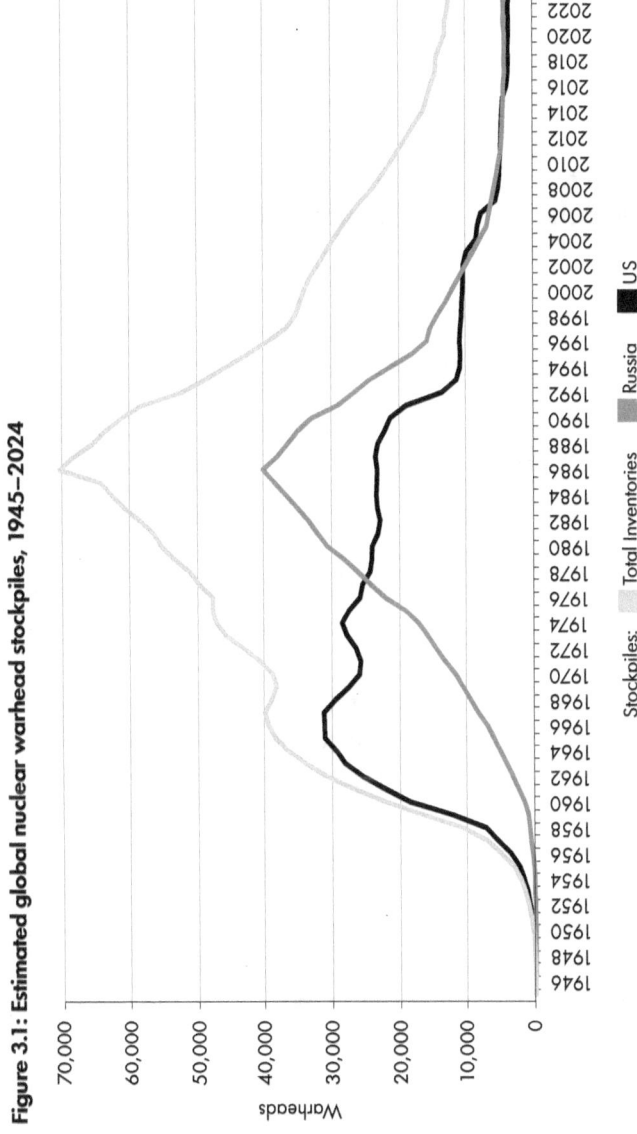

Figure 3.1: Estimated global nuclear warhead stockpiles, 1945–2024

Like the US, the Soviet Union throughout the 1950s continued to develop its military capability and enhance its nuclear stockpile. Demonstrating power and influence in space became increasingly important, too. In 1957, the Soviet Union launched its first Sputnik satellite, and in so doing, presented the image to the West that it was technologically superior in missile technology. In 1959, the Soviets launched the Strategic Rocket Forces as a separate branch of their armed forces and entered into operational service long-range missiles, the Bison and the Bear.

The UK (1952)

The US's partner in the Manhattan Project, the UK, successfully developed its own nuclear capability in 1952. Its involvement in the Manhattan Project meant that it emerged from the war already effectively the 'world's second atomic power', at least *in potentia*.[9] But while it possessed nuclear expertise, it did not have the means to produce the weapon. Delayed by the debilitating costs of the war, the Attlee government approved the UK nuclear programme (1947). Faced with the possibility that the Soviet Union would target the UK in future conflict, it justified the programme as essential to prevent another 'total or general war by producing the means to instigate war'.[10] The UK's 1952 Global Strategy, produced after the re-election of Winston Churchill in 1951, reduced the UK's conventional rearmament spending, focusing instead on atomic weapons to deter potential war with the

Soviet Union.[11] It marked a recognition for the UK that it could not rely on its close relationship with the US; at such a time of distrust and uncertainty, it required atomic weapons.

France (1960)

France's nuclear programme began in 1945. The public were scarred by the years of German occupation and French policy makers wished to acquire a home-grown nuclear capability that would ensure France could react independently to any threats it may face. In 1960 it successfully tested a nuclear device and in 1964 put its first nuclear bomber squadron of Mirage IV into service. Among French defence strategists, there were concerns that the US would not defend Europe against a Soviet or Warsaw Pact attack using conventional means. As Beatrice Heuser noted: 'Who can be sure that in an hour of peril … a President of the United States would … risk having New York or Chicago destroyed in order to save Hamburg or Copenhagen?'[12] This underlying uncertainty has been thought to be the rationale for France's nuclear deterrent policy of strategic autonomy, leading to its withdrawal from NATO's Integrated Military Command in 1966, which it re-joined in 2009. French strategists have argued that nuclear weapons preserve the country's independence and national sovereignty: 'France does not need to rely on any other countries "nuclear umbrella" to ensure its own security.'[13]

China (1964)

When nuclear weapons were used in 1945, Chinese strategists reasoned that 'despite the bombs' awesome destructive power, a politically mobilised conventional fighting force could still defeat an opponent armed with nuclear weapons. ... An atomic weapon was nothing more than an advanced technology that could be overcome through politically mobilised human willpower.'[14] Mao Zedong once famously described nuclear weapons as 'paper tigers' but he recognized that nuclear weapons had enormous military utility, and believed China's development of these weapons was necessary in order to eliminate nuclear threats and the West's nuclear monopoly.

China began its weapons programme in 1955, after the Korean War. Chinese strategists chose to align with the Soviet Union to counter threats from the West. The Sino-Soviet Treaty of 1950 provided China with military and technical assistance, including nuclear assistance. Cracks started to appear in this agreement in the late 1950s due to differing interpretations of Marxism-Leninism between Khrushchev and Mao, and Sino-Soviet co-operation ended in the early 1960s, but by then, China was well on the way to developing a nuclear weapons programme that ensured its strategic independence.

China exploded its first nuclear weapon in October 1964. Following this first test, China released two policies (*zhengce*); the first was a no first use pledge, and the second, an assertion of its commitment to arms control.

In the increasingly fraught decades of the Cold War, there is no doubt that nuclear weapons did help to secure the peace. This was not, however, the full story. The arms race meant that a huge military industry had developed around the fear of nuclear war. Nuclear weapons symbolized the ideological and political differences between Eastern and Western powers, but they were only one element of the Cold War story. The importance of these weapons was promoted to meet political and military objectives. During these early Cold War years, nuclear weapons were tools of status and power, constituting leverage for the few states that possessed them. While they were essentially political and strategic tools to deter aggression, the more weapons that were produced and the more states which had this capability, the greater the probability that they might somehow be used by accident or miscalculation. Any peace was uneasy. The world was getting more dangerous.

4
TABOOS AND STIGMAS

Is it purely the destructive effects of nuclear weapons that make them exceptional, or is there a moral element too? In this chapter I look further into the significance of the development of thermonuclear weapons in shaping moral considerations surrounding the nuclear threat. Throughout the 1950s and 1960s, government decision-makers and military planners in the US, Europe and Soviet Union became increasingly aware of the consequences of the use of nuclear weapons. As has been noted, these more powerful weapons were used as tools in the political brinkmanship of the early Cold War period, but their significance went beyond this. During this time, it became widely understood that any use of these weapons would lead to catastrophic destruction and that, in the event of a nuclear war, only a small percentage of the population were likely to survive. Such knowledge triggered a moral response to these weapons; as the architects of nuclear planning reacted to the nuclear threat, so too did the general public.

The chapter will examine the theoretical arguments about the moral dimension of nuclear weapons. Referring to the 1948 categorization of nuclear weapons, along with chemical and biological weapons, under the term 'Weapons of Mass Destruction' (WMDs), I argue that this categorization is synonymous with a broader stigma towards all three types.[1] The stigma has emerged and developed as a result of entirely understandable concerns about human survival. This has come about slowly over time, as greater knowledge of the full effects of each of these weapons has emerged. Historically, earlier condemnation of chemical and biological weapons established the moral basis for the condemnation of nuclear weapons.

The evidence of this is the nuclear taboo rooted in predominantly Western democratic principles of international law and justice. The taboo is the belief that no state will be the first to use nuclear weapons. The taboo does not address retaliatory nuclear policy, which is deemed to be justifiable, but is only focused on first use.

The nuclear taboo has gradually emerged since 1945, as awareness of the effects of these weapons has increased. I view the civil defence programmes that ran throughout the 1950s in the UK and US as evidence of the seeds of the taboo as widespread publicity of the nuclear threat increased awareness of the dangerous nature of these weapons. The public were told how to prepare for the possibility of nuclear war, effectively bringing this threat into their everyday lives. In time, civil defence programmes were abandoned as knowledge of the repercussions of the use of nuclear weapons increased. With this came the acceptance that there could be no effective protection against a large-scale nuclear war. The public were also reminded of this through film and media portrayals of such an event.

Film and graphic photographic evidence of the environmental destruction caused by the US Bikini Atoll nuclear tests, conducted between 1946 and 1958, provided additional knowledge of the full consequences of the use of nuclear weapons. Slowly, media reports and images of the destruction from these tests spread to the public.

Finally, growing concern about the threat of nuclear war was compounded by the Cuban Missile Crisis in October 1962. This is probably the closest that the world has ever come to nuclear war. On 14 October, nuclear missiles were detected off the coast of Cuba, 90 miles from the US coastline of Florida. The US took this as a provocative move by the Soviet Union and a direct threat. It demanded that the Soviet Union withdraw its weapons, resulting in a nuclear standoff. The world held its breath, fearing that the crisis would lead to nuclear war. Fourteen days later, after direct communication and negotiations between Kennedy and Khrushchev, the crisis was averted when the Soviet Union withdrew its missiles. Such a crisis was televised for the world to see as the threat of nuclear war almost became a reality. When addressing the moral reaction to nuclear weapons, this event was important in two ways. First, it bought the threat of nuclear war into people's everyday lives; it was reminder that what the civil defence guidance had warned of could become reality. Second, both the US and Soviet Union had the ability to use their nuclear weapons and they chose not to. Was this purely due to strategic considerations, or could this also have been because of a human, moral reaction to the consequences of this? I believe this was early evidence of the nuclear taboo.

Norms: stigmatizing weapons of war

A stigma is the process of marking out groups of people, or a social behaviour, as *different* and outside of society. This exclusion as *different* then leads to shaming and/or isolation. The concept of stigma can also be applied in a broader sense to weapons of war. Nuclear weapons stand out as first among equals, alongside chemical and biological weapons, as distinct. While all three may seem very different, they all have the potential to cause long-lasting deadly contamination which provokes a deep moral revulsion and in turn leads to condemnation. The sociologist Erving Goffman[2] identified stigma as a relational concept and one that is subject to change. There are two faces to stigma: that of the stigmatized (seen as *others*) and that of society at large. Stigma forms as a reactionary process between the two.

Throughout history, there have been attempts to limit specific practices of war which are viewed as unjust and morally abhorrent. These efforts have often been driven by strategic objectives and anxiety about the development of increasingly deadly weaponry. In Chapter 2, we saw international efforts to limit the destructiveness of war as a result of developments in weapons technology. The roots of these concerns are addressed here. The stigmatization of chemical, biological and nuclear weapons first manifested through underlying religious sentiment towards war, which was connected to religious principles and teaching.

The Old Testament issued admonitions prohibiting certain acts, such as the slaughter of captured men and the ill-treatment of women and children in war.[3] In the 7th century, the Saracens introduced rules for the conduct of warfare founded on the teachings of the Koran. These forbade the use of early incendiary weapons, the poisoning of wells and the destruction of the enemy's forests.

The Catholic Church attempted to intervene in times of siege. Siege during the Middle Ages affected whole populations, not just the military, subjecting the civilian population to starvation and disease. Pope Innocent II, for example, denounced 'instruments of war which launched projectiles'.[4]

The Christian church and writings of Saint Thomas Aquinas in the 13th century about the morality of war provide what is commonly recognized as the ground rules for Just War Theory. This is the framework used to evaluate whether a war can be morally justified. Just War Theory consists of the twin principles of justice of going to war (*jus ad bellum*) and justice during the conduct of war (*jus in bello*). The former 'requires us to make judgments about aggression and self-defence'.[5] The latter is about the proportionality of the use of force in war and the targeting of combatants (legitimate targets) and non-combatants (civilians) in war. It stipulates that the use of force must be proportional and necessary to meet its objectives.

Stigmatizing weapons of mass destruction

Moral opprobrium towards the use of chemical and biological weapons dates back centuries and forms the basis for moral attitudes towards nuclear weapons. Biological weapons are defined as '[e]ither microorganisms like virus, bacteria or fungi, or toxic substances produced by living organisms that are produced and released deliberately to cause disease and death in humans, animals or plants'.[6] The use of biological weapons is first recorded in the 14th century, when Tatar armies catapulted plague-infected cadavers into enemy cities.[7] Siege machines hurling infectious material into besieged cities are mentioned in accounts of the siege of Thun L'Évêque (1340), Caffa (1346), Karlstein (1422) and Reval (1710).[8]

Chemical weapons are defined as 'a chemical used to cause intentional death or harm through its toxic properties'.[9] Such weapons attack the body in one of four ways: choking agents, blood agents, blister agents and nerve agents. Examples of the use of chemical agents in warfare can be dated back to 429 BCE, when the Spartans are recorded as using noxious smoke on the Athenian allied city Plataia during the Peloponnesian War. In 500 BCE, the Manu Laws of India forbade the use of poisons and other weapons which were considered 'unjustly inhumane'.[10] Chapter 7, Verse 90 states: 'When he fights with his foes in battle, let him not strike with weapons concealed (in wood), nor with (such as are) barbed, poisoned, or the points of which are blazing with fire.'[11]

As I mentioned in Chapter 1, chemical and biological weapons were banned under the Geneva Protocol. The agreement to ban them was prompted by evidence of the devastating effects of the use of chemical weapons during the First World War. While the cult Aum Shinrikyo used chemical weapons and tried to use biological weapons on the Tokyo subway in 1995, their efforts failed and, to date, biological weapons remain a hypothetical threat.

At 5pm on 22 April 1915, the German army released chlorine gas onto the Allied line defending the city of Ypres. Witness accounts described how 'greenish-yellow clouds arose from the enemy's line'. Within a minute, thousands of troops were blanketed in a thick green cloud, blinding them, stopping them from breathing and eventually poisoning many to death. This one attack killed 5,000 men and wounded 10,000.[12] Chemical weapons continued to be used by both sides throughout the rest of the war until 1918. While some protection against these weapons was devised in the form of primitive face pads and gas masks, the physical and psychological harm caused by these attacks was extreme. As the effects of chemical weapons slowly became known, public revulsion towards these weapons grew. After the war, one of the largest public protest movements was the Women's International League for Peace and Freedom, founded in The Hague in 1915; this campaigned against further mobilization of chemical weapons throughout the 1920s and 1930s. The campaign was led by the women who had witnessed the sickening after-effects of the use of chemical weapons during the war and had lost loved ones to them. Their protest contributed to the League of Nations' adoption of the Geneva Protocol.

International action against chemical and biological weapons acted as a precursor for the taboo that followed the use of nuclear weapons in Japan in 1945. The catastrophic effects of the bombings, as well as awareness of the radioactive poisoning suffered by the people of Hiroshima and Nagasaki, reaffirmed and expanded the WMD stigma. This led to the UN categorization of chemical, biological and nuclear weapons as WMD in 1948, defining these as 'atomic explosive weapons, radio-active material weapons, lethal chemical and biological weapons and *any weapons developed in the future which have characteristics comparable in destructive effect to those of the atomic bomb* or other weapons mentioned above' (emphasis my own).[13] This term is inherently a manifestation of the stigma.

The public aversion to the use of nuclear weapons is the result of a socially formed taboo. A standard of practice – a norm – has developed against the use of these weapons. Norms are 'standards of appropriate behaviour for actors of a given identity';[14] they determine practices as morally right or wrong, and are formed over time through the reaction of society to certain practices. This reaction generally begins as small, localized protest. The objection to a certain practice is promoted by activists, campaigning at grassroots level for awareness and action. In time, it becomes a national issue. The norm then cascades, as result of activism and increased international awareness, to be adopted at an international level into the laws of international organizations. A taboo is considered a 'particularly forceful kind of global prohibition'.[15]

The nuclear taboo seriously decreases the likelihood that nuclear weapons will be used as a first resort option, due to moral concerns about the way these weapons kill, and the long-lasting damage that their use causes. I am not the first to argue in favour of nuclear taboo. The academic, Nina Tannenwald, has written extensively about this, arguing that 'at its core is the belief that nuclear weapons, because of their immense destructive power, flagrantly violate long-standing moral principles of discrimination and proportionality in the use of force'.[16]

The public: awareness campaigns in the US

Public awareness of and concern about the nuclear threat first emerged in the late 1940s when the US was the sole nuclear power. From 1949 to 1952, the American public still believed that the nuclear threat could be contained. After the development of thermonuclear weapons (1952 onwards), civil defence programmes were abandoned, acknowledging that survival against a large-scale nuclear attack was impossible.

Starting from when the atomic bombs were used on Japan, governments in the US and Europe used public awareness campaigns to promote the belief that a nuclear attack was survivable. They compared an attack to the air raids of the Second World War and stressed that if the public sheltered from an attack in time, they could survive it. In reality, this was extremely unlikely.

After the Soviet Union developed the atomic bomb, the US passed the Federal Civil Defence Act in 1950, which was designed to 'protect life and property in the United States in case of enemy assault'.[17] This made civil defence the responsibility of individual states. The federal government provided grants to states for the creation of air raid shelters and the stockpiling of food, water and first aid supplies in the event of a nuclear attack. The Act led to the creation of the Civil Defence Administration to oversee a countrywide programme to reassure the public that they could withstand a nuclear attack. The true effects of nuclear weapons were censored due to alarm over the possibility of public hysteria. Propaganda and educational materials were produced to encourage states to invest in nuclear civil defence.

In 1951, the 'Duck and Cover' public education campaign told US citizens how to respond in the event of a nuclear attack. Posters and short films portrayed an animated turtle, Burt, hiding in his shell. The campaign reminded children that they could survive in such a situation if they hid under a desk, against a wall, or ideally, in an air raid shelter. The US was not alone in producing campaigns of this kind. In the Soviet Union, similar material was produced, encouraging citizens to take cover and to use shelters. They were also told to stockpile food and water.

Civil defence experts estimated that a possible attack on the US would come from Soviet planes located in Cuba, 90 miles from Florida. Soviet bombers would fly north, over the Arctic, and attack the US from the north, targeting major cities and densely populated areas. It was feared that biological and chemical weapons might also be used. Such an attack could potentially involve 20-megaton hydrogen bombs (it was thought that this was the most advanced of the Soviet weaponry). There would be no chance of human survival: 'the blast and heat from these bombs would incinerate the cities and their infrastructures instantly, destroying homes 2 miles from the point of detonation, and ignite secondary fires at distances of 30 to 40 miles. Radioactive fallout would travel hundreds of miles in the prevailing winds'.[18]

During the 1950s and 1960s, popular culture in the US frequently featured storylines that addressed the nuclear threat. Television shows such as *Felix the Cat*, *Looney Tunes* and *Space Patrol* included episodes about nuclear weapons.[19] All of these stories emphasized the survivability of an attack. Public information pamphlets such as the December 1961 publication 'Fallout Protection: What to Know and Do about Nuclear Attack' stated that:

> There is no panacea for protection from nuclear attack. In a major attack upon our country, millions of people will be killed. There appears to be no practical programme that would avoid large-scale loss of life. But an effective program of civil defence could save the lives of millions who would not otherwise survive.[20]

While information of this kind was intended to foster public resilience towards the threat of nuclear war, awareness of this dreadful possibility also increased public fear and concern, embedding the nuclear stigma.

UK defence: four-minute warning ...

From 1945 to 1952, UK civil defence programmes were similar to those of the Second World War. The public were urged to comply out of duty, nationalism and a sense of responsibility. In 1949 the UK government called for volunteers to join the Civil Defence Corps, created to organize and train civilians to provide support services in the event of a nuclear attack. After a public campaign in 1952, a call for recruits at local, regional and national level recruited 20,000 members.[21]

In 1952, it was estimated that it would take four minutes from detection of a Soviet nuclear attack to impact. A year later, the Royal Observer Corps established monitoring posts across the UK to provide early warning of enemy aircraft. By the mid-1950s there were 1,500 posts in place.[22]

In 1954, the UK formed a special committee of civil servants to investigate the effects of the use of nuclear weapons; this produced the Strath Report, which stated that, should the UK face a nuclear attack, 'half the population would be killed, major cities laid waste and the rest of the country and its people subject to enough radioactive fallout as to contaminate huge areas and kill millions more. Agriculture and communications would be devastated and the economy destroyed'.[23]

The report called for a radical overhaul of the civil defence services: civil defence needed to have higher priority in defence planning. Public discussion of nuclear weapons and civil defence, it advised, should also be suppressed to avoid civil unrest hysteria. Winston Churchill, in his final address to Parliament in March 1955, argued that, with the development of the hydrogen bomb, '[a] vast quantity of information, some true, some exaggerated, much out of proportion, has been published about the hydrogen bomb. The truth has inevitably been mingled with fiction, and I am glad to say that panic has not occurred. Panic would not necessarily make for peace'. He urged that discussion about the effects of nuclear weapons and the dangers of nuclear war should be kept away from the general public.[24]

The Strath Report shocked politicians and government officials. The incoming prime minister, Anthony Eden, commissioned new war headquarters, where leading political and military figures could seek protection from an attack in a network of underground bunkers, enabling the decision-making functions of the country to go on, despite the devastation. It was not logistically possible to provide such shelter for the general public.

In 1957 the UK established the UK Warning and Monitoring Organisation, which was staffed by Royal Observer Corps full-time and volunteer personnel and run by the Home Office. It was responsible for processing data on nuclear explosions from around the world and forecasting fallout from any nuclear explosion. It operated through the coordination of nuclear warning systems, consisting of warning sirens, monitoring posts and radar technology. In order to address the possibility of a Soviet attack by intercontinental ballistic missiles, the UK signed an agreement with the US in 1963 to host part of their intercontinental ballistic missiles radar system in the UK at the Fylingdales air force base.

The developing stigma: Bikini Atoll

Despite domestic efforts to address the threat of nuclear war and reassure the public that preparedness would save lives, media and news coverage projected a different message. Photographic evidence and reporting made plain the devastation that had been caused by US nuclear tests. This reporting weakened public confidence that nuclear war was survivable.

Bikini Atoll reef is one of a collection of small, inhabited Marshall Islands in the Pacific Ocean. Between 1946 and 1958, the US Joint Navy–Army task force conducted 23 tests on the coral reef, in the sea, in the air and underground. All inhabitants of the Marshall Islands, which included the islands of Rongelap, Utirik, Ujelang and Likiep, were relocated away from the testing sites.

Figure 4.1: Mushroom cloud with ships below during Operation Crossroads nuclear weapons test on Bikini Atoll, July 1946

The first series of tests in 1946 were called 'Operation Crossroads'. These showed that nuclear destruction was greater than anticipated. Public awareness of this grew over time. Ten years later, tests were conducted to measure the effects of the use of thermonuclear weapons on the islands. The biggest of these was Castle Bravo (1954), which caused complete ruin and devastation. After the tests the island of Bikini Atoll was rendered uninhabitable, as were the neighbouring islands of Rongelap, Rongerik, Utirik, Ujelang and Likiep.[25] The thermonuclear weapons caused 'a crater 2 kilometers wide and 80 meters deep.'[26] All wildlife and vegetation was wiped out.

The physical devastation was clear. However, the long-term radiation poisoning would take years to discover. The island was reduced to a radioactive wasteland and those who had been living on it before the tests were made homeless, so-called 'Pacific nomads'. During the 1960s the media began to broadcast this. Those who tried to return to the island suffered radiation poisoning. The inhabitants of Bikini Atoll campaigned for years for compensation for the impact of the tests. During the 1970s scientific studies confirmed high rates of cancer and thyroid illnesses among the islanders.

The devastation of the island was captured on film. The Joint Navy–Army task force carried more than 100 still cameras and 18 tons of film, which was stored in the national archives. In 1946, few televisions existed and images of the tests were shown in newsreels in cinemas or in newspapers. This dissemination increased as time went on and more information became available about the tests. The most famous photographic image is the iconic mushroom cloud image, which has been reproduced throughout the world ever since, creating an association of nuclear weapons with apocalyptic destruction. This imagery, too, reinforced the stigma and emergence of the nuclear taboo.

Heightened fear of war

The closest the world has ever come to all-out nuclear war thus far occurred during the 13 days of the Cuban Missile Crisis. The crisis had been brewing for some time. The Soviet Union and Cuba had formed an ever-closer alliance. Cuba, led by Fidel Castro, was a communist state, which made US leaders anxious that communist ideology would spread to the US. In 1961, the US had conducted a failed military operation to overthrow the Castro government (the Bay of Pigs). That same year, Jupiter missiles, designed to carry nuclear warheads, had been stationed in Italy and Turkey as part of a NATO deterrence strategy. As a reciprocal response to NATO, in July 1962 Castro agreed to host Soviet nuclear weapons on Cuban soil, posing a direct threat to the US. President Kennedy warned that the Soviet Union would face 'the gravest of consequences' for doing so.[27]

On 14 October 1962, US spy planes captured images of Soviet missiles sites in Cuba. These showed medium-range ballistic missiles capable of carrying nuclear ballistic missile warheads with a range of

1,000 nautical miles, which would reach locations such as Washington, DC, the Panama Canal and any other city in the southeastern part of the US. The satellite images also showed that, while not yet operational, the Soviets planned to also station in Cuba intermediate-range ballistic missiles capable of striking most of the major cities in the Western hemisphere. President Kennedy broadcast an address to the nation on 22 October 1962, in which he stated that the Soviet actions constituted an explicit threat to peace and US security. In response he placed his military forces, conventional and nuclear, on their highest level of alert throughout the crisis. US B-52 bombers flew a continuous series of 24-hour flights: '57 bombers and 61 tankers were airborne, 49 of the B-52's, with 182 nuclear weapons aboard were on station, ready for execution orders. ... In addition, 672 bombers and 381 tankers, with a total of 1627 nuclear weapons on board, were on station, ready for execution orders.'[28] The following days saw intense diplomatic efforts to stop the crisis. The Executive Committee of the National Security Council debated a range of options, including diplomatic and covert actions, a naval blockade, airstrikes, a full invasion of Cuba, political and public messaging, and diplomatic backchannel negotiations.

On day seven, 22 October, Kennedy implemented a naval blockade of Cuba, preventing any movement in or out of the island. In a live television broadcast to the American public, he said:

> [W]e no longer live in a world where only the actual firing of weapons represents a sufficient challenge to a nation's national security to constitute maximum peril. Nuclear weapons are so destructive and ballistic missiles are so swift, that any substantially increased possibility of their use or any sudden change in their deployment may well be regarded as a definite threat to peace.[29]

Kennedy called on Khrushchev to remove the weapons in Cuba. Khrushchev wrote to Kennedy the following day stating that nuclear weapons were purely to 'deter an attack on Cuba', and had been stationed there as a result of NATO stationing nuclear Jupiter missiles in Italy and Turkey. The US-imposed blockade was a violation of international norms of freedom of navigation.[30]

Diplomatic efforts continued throughout the next few days. The US turned to the UN, presenting proof of the Soviet weapons in Cuba. Eventually, Khrushchev wrote to Kennedy on 26 October stating that the missiles would be removed, 'under United Nations supervision and inspection' and in exchange the US would remove the 'quarantine' (blockade) and pledge not to invade Cuba.[31]

Crisis had been averted. Did deterrence really work? Or was it down to the nuclear stigma? The truth is most likely to be a mixture of strategic, political, diplomatic and moral factors. The crisis had been a wake-up call and a reminder of how real the nuclear threat was.

5
NON-PROLIFERATION, ARMS CONTROL AND POPULAR PROTEST

Is the purpose of nuclear weapons to force politicians and the public to consider broader issues of humanity, social justice and environmental safety? That of course was not why they were created, but it can be seen as one of their effects. To what extent did moral factors alter Cold War strategic policy?

The moral dimension of nuclear weapons is evidenced in the political and diplomatic work after the use of nuclear weapons in 1945, to establish a nuclear non-proliferation regime. This grew into a legal framework of international agreements to limit the proliferation of nuclear weapons. These included attempts to stop nuclear weapons testing (1963) and limit the fissile materials required to develop nuclear weapons (1964). While the motivations for a non-proliferation regime could initially be seen as an effort by the US to secure a strategic advantage and prevent more states from acquiring nuclear weapons, as time went by and more states acquired them, this reasoning no longer was valid. Diplomatic efforts to address the proliferation and use of nuclear weapons continued. Moral concerns certainly played a part in this decision-making.

The most successful product of the non-proliferation regime was the NPT (1970): while previous efforts to ban nuclear testing and conclude a Fissile Material Cut-off Treaty only had partial success, the NPT has withstood the test of time and is still an important treaty today. The treaty limits the spread of nuclear weapons and its signatories pledge to work towards nuclear disarmament. In 2025, 191 states have acceded to the NPT, a clear sign of its success. The treaty accepts that a handful of states, the US (1945), the Soviet Union (1949), UK (1952), France (1960) and China (1964), can keep their nuclear weapons; all other states must agree not to manufacture or acquire nuclear weapons. In exchange, non-nuclear weapon states (NNWS) receive shared scientific knowledge to enable the development of the peaceful uses of nuclear energy. The treaty's main limitation is the division between nuclear weapon states (NWS) and NNWS, which creates inescapable tension. The NWS are also the permanent five members of the UN Security Council. Despite this, the treaty goes a long way to preventing the further proliferation of nuclear weapons.

In addition to legal efforts to prevent nuclear proliferation, public awareness of the nuclear threat continued to increase throughout the latter half of the Cold War. Film and television programmes played their part, by dramatizing a nuclear future. *The Day After* (Russell J. Oakes, 1983) and *When the Wind Blows* (Jimmy Murakami, 1986) portrayed the effects of the use of nuclear weapons and documented the apocalyptic consequences of this.

Public anxiety manifested in global anti-nuclear protest movements driven by concerns about intentional and accidental nuclear war and nuclear accidents. Throughout the late 1960s and 1970s protest movements such as the Federation of American Scientists, Greenpeace and the Campaign for Nuclear Disarmament advanced public awareness about the dangers of nuclear weapons and urged leaders to disarm. These campaigns pushed for a complete eradication of nuclear weapons. While addressing the specific dangers of nuclear weapons, these movements also spotlighted broader issues of humanity, social justice and environmental concerns. Driving anti-nuclear protests were a number of global nuclear accidents, including Three Mile Island in Pennsylvania (1979) and Chernobyl in Ukraine (1986). Public concern about the safety of civilian nuclear sites led to increased public protest.

This chapter examines diplomatic attempts to stem the spread of nuclear weapons, as well as the growing influence of anti-nuclear protest movements. I identify that the normative attitudes towards nuclear weapons had evolved, leading to the embedding of the taboo, confirming that moral considerations throughout the 1950s, 1960s and 1970s did alter Cold War strategic policy.

The US-led Baruch Plan (1946), named after Bernard Baruch, the US representative to the UN at the time, proposed that the US (then the sole nuclear power) decommission its nuclear weapons and agree to nuclear safeguards. These included the establishment of a central body to oversee atomic energy activities worldwide, international inspections of atomic energy sites and a system of reporting, whereby states with nuclear programmes would be required to provide full accounts of their nuclear activities. Any violation of these safeguards would be subject to international sanctions imposed by the UN member states.

In exchange for the US giving up its weapons capability, Baruch sought agreement that all other states would not pursue nuclear weapons.[1] When the Soviet Union developed nuclear weapons in 1949, it became evident that US unilateral disarmament would not be possible. While the Baruch Plan had failed to progress, the safeguarding provisions within it would prove to be of importance in the future.

An article in the *Daily Mail* in September 1949 summed up the anxieties of the time, referring to the Soviet Union's successful atomic test and asking,

> Does this mean that now the two great giants, the U.S.A and U.S.S.R. are at last on equal terms a clash must follow – one or the other calculating to "get the blow in first"? Not necessarily. *First*, we have to be convinced that the Russians want war. Or even believe that it is inevitable

despite their dogma? ... Marxism teaches that there must be a final clash with Capitalism before Communism can be established. ... *Second,* the Russians place great reliance on undermining Capitalist States by the methods of the Cold War. ... *Third,* we do not ourselves maintain that the two giants, once equally armed must necessarily fight. ... *Yet, the sobering thought remains that men are like little children playing with a most deadly weapon. Something terrible may indeed happen unless they grow up – FAST!*[2]

Political and diplomatic efforts did continue after this to establish a non-proliferation regime. These included agreements to halt the production of materials required to develop nuclear weapons, the testing of nuclear devices and the further proliferation of these weapons. It was thought that if all of these agreements could be achieved, they would prevent nuclear war.

In the early stages, throughout the 1950s, the Soviet Union's negotiating position favoured establishing atomic-free zones and a comprehensive ban on nuclear testing. However, despite this, Soviet public statements indicated a growing sense of 'ambivalence towards the whole question of proliferation'.[3]

An additional motivation for these diplomatic initiatives was concern about the global availability of uranium, noted in Chapter 2. Uranium needs to be mined and, in the 1940s, it was thought that there were few sites where this could take place – the Belgian Congo, Canada, Czechoslovakia and the US (Colorado, Utah and Wyoming). After 1950, the discovery of larger uranium deposits in Kazakhstan, Canada, South Africa, Australia and the US eased these concerns.

Between 1951 and 1958, the US conducted 188 nuclear tests, the Soviet Union 82 and the UK 21.[4] As mentioned in the previous chapter, nuclear testing posed a significant danger to public health and had a catastrophic effect on the environment. In 1958, Irish delegate Frank Aiken, his country's Minister for External Affairs, speaking at the 13th session of the UN General Assembly, called for a historic landmark suspension of nuclear weapons tests. Aiken proposed that rather than trying to achieve an 'all time' agreement to ban weapons testing, favoured by the Soviet Union, efforts should focus on a short-term agreement, possibly for as little as a year. Aiken made an impassioned plea that delaying agreement could lead to more states acquiring nuclear weapons. He proposed that non-nuclear states should 'refrain from manufacturing or acquiring nuclear weapons' and urged nuclear states to:

> refrain from supplying such weapons to states which do not now possess them. ... If we do not soon succeed in limiting the number of states making or possessing nuclear weapons, the problem of saving the world from nuclear destruction may well have passed beyond the power of man to solve.[5]

Aiken warned about the danger of nuclear weapons to humanity and was concerned that they might fall into the hands of irresponsible states:

> All through history portable weapons which are the monopoly of the great powers today become the weapons of smaller powers and revolutionary groups tomorrow. And since local wars and revolutions almost always involve some degree of great power patronage and rivalry, the use of nuclear weapons by a small state or revolutionary group could lead, only too easily, to the outbreak of general war. One obsolete, Hiroshima-type bomb, used by a small and desperate country to settle a local quarrel, could be the detonator for world-wide thermo-nuclear war, involving the destruction of our whole civilization.[6]

Power and prestige would drive states to acquire these weapons; these same factors might also drive them to use them. Efforts to limit testing and to control the supply of nuclear materials would go some way to limit these dangers.

Aiken's speech increased global pressure to limit nuclear testing. The speech also lent momentum to anti-nuclear peace movements. It paved the way for further discussions at the UN, which led to the establishment of a subcommittee on nuclear weapons testing.

On 5 August 1963, the US, Soviet Union and the UK finally reached an agreement on a Partial Test Ban Treaty, prohibiting the testing of nuclear weapons above ground, in outer space or underwater. Underground testing was permitted, but it was agreed that the radioactive debris from any such explosion must be contained within the territorial limits of the state conducting the test.

Advancement towards preventing the spread of nuclear materials was harder to achieve. In 1964, President Lyndon B. Johnson proposed at the Eighteen Nation Committee on Disarmament a freeze on the nuclear arms race and a separate Fissile Material Cut-Off Treaty.[7] Despite early progress, the heightened political tensions of the time meant that controlling the spread of nuclear materials was very difficult to achieve and multilateral attempts towards a fissile material cut-off were abandoned. These were only resurrected years later, in 1993, but once again failed to progress due to disagreement regarding verification.

The appeal of nuclear energy

Ever since Otto Hahn and Fritz Strassmann split the atom, scientists have been working to harness nuclear energy for peaceful purposes. The first nuclear reactor to generate electricity was developed in 1951 in Idaho, US. On 8 December 1953, US President Dwight Eisenhower presented the Atoms for Peace speech to the UN General Assembly, calling for the establishment of an international agency to pool scientific knowledge about nuclear energy. Eisenhower argued that:

> The United States knows that if the fearful trend of atomic military build-up can be reversed, this greatest of destructive forces can be developed into a great boon, for the benefit of all mankind. The United States knows that peaceful power from atomic energy is no dream of the

> future. The capability, already proved, is here today. Who can doubt that, if the entire body of the world's scientists and engineers had adequate amounts of fissionable material with which to test and develop their ideas, this capability would rapidly be transformed into universal, efficient and economic usage?[8]

The full potential of nuclear energy was as yet untested and, as a result, it seemed to hold out the promise of revolutionizing industry and improving living conditions at a time when many states were trying to recover and rebuild after the devastation of the Second World War. Scientific advances in nuclear energy could lead to innovative ways to boost food production and scientific advances in nuclear energy could provide advances in science. Eisenhower's Atoms for Peace plan sought to capitalize on this. In 1957, the International Atomic Energy Agency (IAEA) was established to provide states with shared knowledge about the development and scientific application of nuclear power.

In order to safely promote the civilian use of nuclear energy, it was important to prevent nuclear misuse and to ensure that nuclear energy programmes were not being adapted to develop nuclear weapons. The IAEA was initially established to 'act as an intermediary for the supply of materials, equipment and services'. It was not able to enforce any safeguarding arrangements on states and requested that states make their own individual arrangements for this.

The Treaty on the Non-Proliferation of Nuclear Weapons (NPT, 1970)

Eisenhower's Atoms for Peace speech and the subsequent establishment of the IAEA opened new diplomatic avenues through which to address the spread of nuclear weapons. By addressing the peaceful uses of nuclear energy, it was possible to look at alternative ways of developing nuclear knowledge, quite separate from a focus upon weapons development. This is exactly what the NPT did.

The NPT was opened for signature in 1968 and entered into force in 1970. It addressed the technology issue by offering non-nuclear states the incentive to join the treaty and receive the benefits of developing or acquiring 'all types of peaceful nuclear technologies' subject to international safeguards.[9] In exchange for this, they would agree never to seek to manufacture or receive nuclear explosives and to pursue negotiations, in good faith, to achieve complete disarmament. The treaty called for the newly established IAEA to be the governing body to ensure verification.

The treaty recognized nuclear weapon states as states that had successfully tested nuclear weapons by 1967. These states, the US, the Soviet Union, China, the UK and France, agreed not to share their nuclear capability and to eventually work towards disarmament in good faith. Members of the NPT are free to leave the treaty at any time, but must give three months' notice of this. The only state to have left the NPT to date is North Korea, in 2003.

The treaty is widely regarded as the most successful non-proliferation agreement. While it created a fundamental division between member states and has not achieved complete disarmament, it has limited nuclear proliferation and provided member states with some level of security and autonomy. Its success is demonstrated by its longevity.

Further progress towards arms control came in 1969, when both the US and Soviet Union, after years of weapons development, agreed to a period of détente. The term détente refers to an easing or relaxing of tensions. By 1969, the race to acquire bigger and more powerful weapons was an economic strain on both superpowers. The Soviet Union had developed its strategic intercontinental military forces to match those of the US, causing alarm in the West. The US was threatening to shift the strategic balance by developing an anti-ballistic missile programme. The Sentinel and Safeguard programmes were initiated in the 1960s to create a defensive shield capable of intercepting and destroying incoming ballistic missiles. The Soviet Union could not match this capability, or the strategic advantage that it provided to US forces. In addition, in Europe, East–West tensions had eased through the diplomatic management of relations, most notably Ostpolitik, which led to improved links between West Germany and Eastern bloc countries. In addition, Sino-Soviet relations had deteriorated.

Détente lasted for a little over a decade. During this period, the Anti-Ballistic Missile Treaty was signed in 1972. Both sides agreed maintaining a maximum of to two anti-ballistic missile sites, later reduced to one, in order to preserve strategic stability and prevent either side from undermining Mutually Assured Destruction. As their name suggests, the purpose of these systems was to shoot down incoming ballistic missiles. The Anti-Ballistic Missile Treaty aimed to prevent a destabilizing arms race in missile defence.

The greatest success of détente was the Strategic Arms Limitation Talks (SALT) agreements. These were a series of talks and treaties aimed at reducing the nuclear threat by addressing the number and size of weapons each side possessed. SALT I (1972) established an Interim Agreement that froze the number of intercontinental ballistic missiles and submarine-launched ballistic missiles at existing levels for five years.

But it did not address strategic bombers or warhead numbers, thus allowing both sides to continue manufacturing nuclear weapons without violating its terms. SALT I was a major step towards stabilizing the risk of nuclear war. While the treaty contained caveats, the agreement of both sides to sit down and discuss the possibility of limiting arms was itself a major step forward.

SALT I was followed by SALT II, which sought to establish a more comprehensive treaty to limit the possession and manufacturing of strategic launchers. Negotiations began in 1972 and, despite agreement in 1979, efforts to finalize the treaty were destroyed by the Soviet invasion of Afghanistan that same year. Despite this, both sides voluntarily adhered to many of its provisions until the mid-1980s. While détente eased tensions between the US and Soviet Union, conflicts continued to exist throughout the 1970s, in Vietnam, Israel, Bangladesh and Cambodia. Nuclear weapons did not prevent these conflicts. Nuclear anxiety still dominated world affairs. While conflict prevailed, the threat of a large-scale nuclear war did prevent all-out superpower confrontation.

People power: public protest

Alongside diplomatic efforts to promote arms control, public protest against nuclear weapons increased. In the late 1950s and early 1960s grassroots movements against nuclear weapons had spread throughout the world, driven by health and environmental concerns associated with nuclear weapons and nuclear weapons testing.

The images of the Bikini Atoll tests, mentioned in the previous chapter, in particular the Castle Bravo test, caused outrage and protest. The author Nina Tannenwald has written that:

> For many in the antinuclear weapons movement, nuclear disarmament was primarily a moral issue. ... One of its main accomplishments was to help shift the perception of nuclear weapons from primarily explosive devices to more insidious implements, more akin to chemical or biological weapons. This was a result of a growing understanding of the long-term effects of radiation exposure and fallout from nuclear testing, disseminated by the efforts of scientists and peace groups.[10]

Research into the effects of radiation poisoning on the civilian population had been under way since the use of atomic weapons in 1945; protest ensued as more information about the full effects of these weapons came out. Despite the IAEA stating that the effects of radiation poisoning were minimal,[11] more and more leading scientists, such as the National Academy of Scientists (1956) and the British epidemiologist Alice Stewart (1958), identified a link between leukaemia, bone cancer and nuclear fallout.[12]

The physicist Ralph Lapp, an early critic of the Castle Bravo test (1954), helped raise awareness about Strontium-90 contamination. Biologist Barry Commoner established the St Louis Committee for Nuclear Information, later named the Committee for Nuclear Information, which focused on measuring radioactive contamination from nuclear tests and played a crucial role in raising public weakness of the dangers to health resulting from nuclear testing. The Committee's 'Baby tooth survey' research (1958–1970) identified increased levels of Strontium-90, a radioactive by-product of nuclear fallout, in children's teeth as a result of atmospheric testing. The preliminary results were published in the leading journal *Science* in 1961. In the US, the National Committee for a Sane Nuclear Policy was established in 1957; many celebrities and public figures, including Martin Luther King, Marilyn Monroe, Arthur Miller, Henry Fonda, Marlon Brando, Harry Belafonte and Ossie Davis, were sponsors to this organization and it conducted a number of high-profile advertising and publicity campaigns for nuclear test ban, arms control and disarmament. These included a full-page *New York Times* ad in 1957 warning about the danger of nuclear testing; it cautioned that 'We are facing a danger unlike any danger that has ever existed.'[13]

Prominent nuclear scientists wrote about the dangers the world faced as a result of nuclear accidents and testing. Linus Pauling won a Nobel Prize in 1962 for his work drawing attention to the health dangers of nuclear testing. He was a driving force in the Pugwash movement, named after the location in Canada where it was established. This played a key role in advocating for arms control agreements, including the Partial Test Ban Treaty (1963).

As greater progress was made towards arms control, public protest quietened down for a time. Many of the fears over nuclear testing were allayed by the signing of the Partial Test Ban Treaty, which, while permitting underground testing, was considered a significant milestone in curbing nuclear testing.

The danger posed by nuclear weapons continued to be portrayed in popular fiction and the media. From the 1950s on, works such as *On the Beach* (Nevil Shute, 1959), *Cat's Cradle* (Kurt Vonnegut, 1963) and the film *The Day the Earth Caught Fire* (Val Guest, 1961) all dealt with life after a nuclear disaster. Television series such as *Twilight Zone* (1959) and *The Outer Limits* (1963) included episodes that imagined possible scenarios of nuclear war. Documentaries and films also highlighted this danger. Peter Watkins' pseudo-documentary *The War Game* (1966) was pulled by the

BBC before its provisional screening date in 1965 due to fears it was too horrifying, as it portrayed the aftermath of a nuclear strike on the UK. It premiered in April 1966 and won an Academy Award in 1967. The 1964 Stanley Kubrick film, *Dr Strangelove: Or How I Learned to Stop Worrying and Love the Bomb*, is considered a satiric masterpiece, portraying the dangers of an accidental nuclear war and showing the irrationality of nuclear decision-makers. The television movie *Red Alert* (William Hale, 1977) displayed images of simultaneous nuclear reactors spiralling out of control.

The 1973–4 energy crisis once again reinvigorated public protest over the danger posed by civilian nuclear energy programmes. The crisis, caused by an embargo by the Arab oil exporting states, the Organization of Arab Petroleum Exporting Countries, meant that oil prices throughout the West and beyond skyrocketed. As a policy to counter Western dependence upon oil, most European states and the US accelerated existing nuclear power programmes to become their top priority, sparking public protest.

NATO's decision in 1979 to station 500 Cruise and Pershing II intermediate-range ballistic missiles on European soil led to mass protest throughout Western Europe, too. This was one of the largest anti-nuclear movements in history. Opinion polls indicated that, while the public was reassured by NATO's deterrence power, they did not want nuclear weapons in their 'neighbourhood'. This, they worried, made them targets for a Soviet Union attack and elevated the possibility of a nuclear accident.[14]

Figure 5.1: Anti-war, anti-nuclear-weapons rally, Wall Street, New York, US, 1981

The Campaign for Nuclear Disarmament, founded in 1957 in London, reported that the stationing of these missiles led to a massive growth in its membership:

> [W]eek by week arrived more letters, more membership applications, more callers, more journalists, more requests for speakers, more orders for badges and leaflets. ... Our two small office rooms, which can't have amounted to more than 300 square feet in total were jammers with volunteers ... by the end of 1980 we were in new offices, themselves becoming too small. New memberships poured in by hundreds every week. The graph we had on the wall outgrew the wall and had to be taken across the ceiling.[15]

Throughout the 1980s, concerns about nuclear energy programmes continued to be overshadowed by the possibility of nuclear war. These concerns were magnified by the breakdown in international relations at the time. Détente between the US and the Soviet Union had broken down and the SALT II talks had ended without agreement.

Popular fiction, film and television series continued to address the prospect of nuclear war. The film *When the Wind Blows* (Jimmy Murakami, 1986), originally a novel published in 1982, written by Raymond Briggs, highlighted the aftermath of a nuclear apocalypse. It features an English couple and their attempts to survive a nearby attack. One scene highlights the unique and terrifying nature of threat clearly:

> Jim: I wonder if there is any radiation about.

> Hilda: Well, I can't see anything.
>
> Jim: Hurry up dear and get back in the Inner Core or Refuge. We'd better have an early night.
>
> Hilda: Well if I can't see it and can't feel it, it can't be doing any harm, can it?

In the UK, the film *The Day After* (Russell J. Oakes, 1983) was broadcast on television. This was followed a year later by the film *Threads* (Mick Jackson, 1984). Both films staged the catastrophic consequences of nuclear war. Opinion polls taken before and after the airing of *The Day After* showed that it had a substantial impact on public perceptions. In particular, the film and the controversy generated after its release had an impact upon the salience of nuclear war. The film stirred up feelings of, and intentions to engage in, anti-nuclear protest, estimates of the probability that a war may occur, and beliefs about the likelihood and desirability of survival.[16]

In studies of the impact of images of nuclear war on the general public, it has been found that concerns about survival dominate. Representation of nuclear war motivates anti-nuclear activity.[17] Throughout the 1980s the protest campaigns intensified. Several factors contributed to this. The first was NATO's decision to place a new generation of nuclear short- and middle-range missiles in Europe. In West Germany in particular the peace movement became the 'paramount social movement'.[18] Josef Joffee notes that 'the Federal Republic came to host more nuclear weapons per square mile than any other nation in the world.

And the bulk of these tactical weapons was short-range, hence destined to devastate the defender's not the aggressor's land'.[19]

Concerns about the safety of civil nuclear energy plants were given new strength after the Three Mile Island nuclear accident in 1979 in Pennsylvania, US. Unit 2 of the Three Mile Island nuclear generating station suffered a partial meltdown due to a combination of mechanical failures and operator errors. Nobody died in this accident, radioactive gases were contained, and it did not lead to significant radiation exposure, but it attracted huge public attention and fed uneasiness about the safety of nuclear reactors.

The largest and most deadly nuclear accident occurred in April 1986, when Reactor No. 4 at the Chernobyl nuclear power plant in the former Ukrainian Republic of the Soviet Union exploded, causing a large fire and releasing large amounts of radiation into the atmosphere. Immediately after the accident, an exclusion zone was created around the nuclear site, which was subsequently expanded when the extent of the contamination became clearer. The IAEA reported that from 27 April to mid-August 1986 about 116,000 people were evacuated from their homes in the region around the plant to protect them from radiation exposure. Over 800 cases of childhood cancer had been reported[20] among young people living in Ukraine and neighbouring Belarus. The UN estimated 50 deaths from the disaster. Richard Gray has written about the experiences of 'liquidators', the Ukrainian professionals working next to the site to clean up the Chernobyl accident. 'In Ukraine, death rates among these brave individuals has soared, rising from 3.5 to 17.5 deaths per 1,000 people between 1988 and 2012.'[21] The Chernobyl nuclear power accident further enhanced fears of the devastation caused by out of control nuclear reactors.

Public protest against nuclear weapons, alongside diplomatic efforts to embed nuclear non-proliferation within international law, demonstrate that moral factors did influence policy. The ethical debates about these weapons were part of growing concern about humanity, social justice and the environment.

6
AFTER THE COLD WAR

The events of 9 November 1989 in Berlin touched the world. Peaceful protests calling for greater freedoms and democratic reform had been taking place for weeks before this in Poland, Hungary, Bulgaria, Czechoslovakia, Romania and East Germany. In May 1989 the Hungarian government dismantled its barbed wire border with Austria. This allowed East Germans to travel to Hungary and escape to West Germany. On 4 June 1989, Poland's Solidarity party won an overwhelming electoral victory leading to the end of communist rule two months later. That summer, communist governments were replaced by democratically elected governments in Hungary and Czechoslovakia.

On 4 November 1989, half a million people had gathered in East Berlin in mass protest against the physical division of the city imposed by the Berlin Wall. On 9 November 1989, protesters rallied near the wall at the Brandenburg Gate. The Berlin Wall, a concrete and barbed wire structure that encircled West Berlin, had been heavily guarded since it was erected in 1961. Many had died attempting to cross it. But on this day, the guards stood aside and allowed the protesters to cross from East to West. This was a historic moment. The brutally enforced division between East and West Germany had been removed.

In a post-Cold War world, what were nuclear weapons for? Was the world entering an era where we would witness the end of nuclear weapons?

In this chapter I look at the nuclear debates in the decade after the fall of the Soviet Union (1990–2001). Conflict remained, as ethnic and cultural divisions, suppressed by the Cold War powers, re-emerged. These led to civil wars in Yugoslavia (1991–2001) and Somalia (1991–ongoing), as well as the Rwanda genocide (1994).

On 29 January 1991, in his State of the Union address, President George H.W. Bush heralded this as a new world order, in which 'diverse nations are drawn together in common cause to achieve the universal aspirations of mankind – peace and security, freedom and the rule of law'.[1] This new world meant new challenges and these would demand new solutions. The newly appointed Secretary General of the UN Boutros Boutros-Ghali, in 1992, called for an emphasis on preventative diplomacy, peace-keeping and peace-making. The hope was that international institutions would play a greater role in world affairs, helping to reduce the power divisions between states and prevent conflict.

While, as we now know, disarmament proved unattainable, significant progress was made to enhance non-proliferation agreements. In particular, the NPT was extended indefinitely. In addition, South Africa ended its nuclear weapons programme (1989) and joined the NPT (1991). Ukraine also signed the Budapest Memorandum in 1994 agreeing to give up its nuclear weapons. In 2003, Libya also announced the dismantling of its nuclear programme.

Despite this progress, the strategic attraction of nuclear weapons remained. For some states, nuclear weapons represented strategic superiority. The Iraqi leader Saddam Hussein's invasion of Kuwait and his pursuit of a nuclear weapons programme are examples of this. India conducted a successful 'peaceful nuclear explosion', Smiling Buddha (Ministry of External Affairs designation: Pokhran-I), on 18 May 1974. However, due to international pressure and political restraints it did not declare itself a nuclear weapons state. It achieved this in 1998. That same year, in response to India's nuclear tests, Pakistan likewise declared itself a nuclear weapons state. The threat of nuclear proliferation had clearly not gone away.

The events in 1989 meant that the future was uncertain. But in George H.W. Bush's State of the Union address quoted earlier, he predicted a future '[w]here diverse nations are drawn together in common cause to achieve the universal aspirations of mankind – peace and security, freedom, and rule of law'.[2] In 1989, Francis Fukuyama famously wrote an article for the *National Interest* entitled 'The End of History', in which he argued that the end of the Cold War had meant a victory for liberal ideology and market capitalism:

> what we are witnessing is not just the end of the cold war, or a passing of a particular period of post-war history, but the end of history as such: that is, the end point of mankind's ideological evolution and the universalisation of western liberal democracy as the final form of human government.[3]

Fukuyama argued that the end of history did not mean the end of conflict. Conflict was still possible, however 'large-scale conflict must involve large states still caught in the grip of history, and they are what appear to be passing from the scene'.[4] Fukuyama developed these ideas into a book in 1992. The tradition which Fukuyama draws on is one which maintains that the human race is progressing and that it is moving towards an end point at which conflict and violence will cease.

Often, when I teach my students about the significance of the end of the Cold War, I use the analogy of the party popper. I try to explain how the religious, cultural and territorial identity of states had, for many, been suppressed within a metaphorical party popper. From the 19th century, throughout the world, tribal and ethnic groups had lost their independence to colonial rule. The Second World War had altered the territorial boundaries of states. New states were created and old territorial boundaries lost.

The end of the Cold War was like the string being pulled on a party popper; you pull the string, the friction causes ignition and the confetti is ejected. Conflict arose in Europe, Africa, Asia and the Middle East due to ethnic, cultural and religious tensions. These were seen in Somalia, Rwanda, Sierra Leone and Yugoslavia. Conflict was localized but none the less bloody.

The world witnessed the atrocities of ethnic cleansing and genocide, nowhere more brutally than the genocide of the civil war (1994) in Rwanda between the Hutus and Tutsis. International attempts to prevent this type of conflict required an altered focus, away from spheres of influence and states, and more towards people and the rights of the individuals. In 2005, the UN members endorsed the Responsibility to Protect doctrine, which maintains that states have a fundamental responsibility to protect their citizens. Should the state fail to do so, the international community has the right to violate the sovereignty of the state to protect people, from genocide, war crimes, ethnic cleansing and crimes against humanity. The threat of nuclear weapons was useless in such conflicts. World events presented the possibility that nuclear weapons could have more value as weapons that states *rejected* than as ones they sought to acquire. The non-proliferation movement that had been so active during the Cold War years was now a focus for the optimism and opportunity created by the end of Soviet system for those states oppressed by its rule. As was to be seen, this was not the case for all.

Despite this new optimism for disarmament, nuclear weapons remained in situ throughout the former Soviet

Union. It is estimated that 35,000 nuclear weapons were sited in former Soviet territory across Eastern and Central Europe, covering a Eurasian land mass that spanned 11 time zones. There was a new danger that nuclear materials could possibly be acquired by criminal networks and terrorist organizations. The Soviet Union's stockpile of 22,000 tactical nuclear weapons was of particular concern.[5]

As well as warheads, other nuclear materials were scattered throughout Ukraine, Belarus and Kazakhstan. While it was extremely unlikely that any terrorist organization could acquire and transport a large nuclear weapon across Europe, it was possible that the materials from such weapons could be transported separately. The danger was that nuclear material could be attached to conventional weapons to create a so-called 'dirty bomb' (radiological weapon).

A separate but simultaneous concern was that states might seek to acquire their own nuclear weapon by obtaining the parts for the nuclear bombs from various sources piecemeal. In an effort to prevent the spread of nuclear materials to potential proliferators, in 1991 US Senators Sam Nunn and Richard Lugar authored legislation for a Co-operative Threat Reduction Programme. This ensured that the US co-ordinated the dismantling and elimination of nuclear weapons, along with other weapons of mass destruction and their infrastructure in former Soviet states. Between 1992 and 1996, the US Congress authorized US$2.458 billion to the programme.[6]

In the aftermath of the Cold War, states developing nuclear weapons programmes were encouraged by the US and UN to relinquish them. In 1989, South Africa's President F.W. de Klerk announced a commitment to dismantle his country's nuclear weapons programme. De Klerk, facing the fall of the apartheid regime, calculated that the benefits of international co-operation outweighed any strategic advantage nuclear weapons might offer. The country had been well on the way to developing its own weapons capability.[7]

The end of the Cold War meant that Ukraine held 15 per cent of the former Soviet nuclear arsenal.[8] Despite this, Ukraine's leaders at the time viewed maintaining this arsenal as a strategic threat. In 1994, Ukraine signed the Budapest Memorandum, transferring all of its nuclear warheads to Russia for elimination. The academic Aldo Zammit Borda has written that:

> In exchange for giving up its nuclear arsenal, Ukraine initially sought legally binding guarantees from the US that it would intervene should Ukraine's sovereignty be breached. But when it became clear that the US was not willing to go that far, Ukraine agreed to somewhat weaker – but nevertheless significant – politically binding security assurances to respect its independence and sovereignty which guaranteed its existing borders.[9]

In 2003, Libya's leader, Muammar Gaddafi, relinquished its weapons of mass destruction programme, which included a nuclear weapons programme. The

Libyan programme had begun in the 1970s, despite membership of the NPT. He viewed nuclear weapons as a symbol of modern statehood and brought in expertise to develop the programme. To Gaddafi, nuclear weapons would give Libya membership of an exclusive club of states. Strategically, Libya lacked effective conventional ground, air and naval forces. Nuclear weapons would change this and greatly elevate Libya's status within the region, countering any threat from Israel's nuclear capability. Libyans estimated that they were five years away from completion of their programme, however we now know that this was an unrealistic assessment. Gaddafi weighed completion of a nuclear weapons programme and the challenges associated with this, against international recognition, economic aid and the removal of sanctions.[10] He chose the latter.

The US also set a trend of downgrading the importance of its nuclear weapons. In 1991, President George H.W. Bush launched a series of nuclear presidential initiatives, which reduced the amount of operational nuclear weapons available to US forces. For the first time since the early part of the Cold War, US bomber planes were taken off high alert.[11]

NATO also adapted to the altered strategic context. It maintained its purpose to guarantee the freedom and security of all members through political and military means. The UK Prime Minister Margaret Thatcher is quoted as saying 'you don't cancel your home insurance policy just because there have been fewer burglaries on your street in the last 12 months'.[12] But NATO also reinvented itself, acting as a co-operative security organization, which meant that its strategic concept altered to emphasize dialogue, cooperation and crisis management. It established a Partnership for Peace in 1994, which included 22 non-NATO states, former Warsaw Pact countries among them. The Partnership for Peace was created to foster military integration, build trust, and encourage democratization and reform. The programme aligned partner states' military forces with NATO standards, provided military training programmes and peacekeeping activities. It still exists today. Russia joined the Partnership in 1994. NATO also expanded its membership in this period, admitting Poland, Hungary and the Czech Republic in 1999. Membership increased again in 2004 when Bulgaria, Estonia, Latvia, Lithuania, Romania, Slovakia and Slovenia joined. In 2009, it expanded again, extending membership to Albania and Croatia. NATO continues to expand its membership, with Montenegro joining in 2017, the Republic of North Macedonia in 2020, Finland in 2023 and Sweden in 2024.

Nuclear weapons redux

While the end of the Cold War saw some states give up their nuclear weapons programmes, others still chose to develop them, believing that nuclear weapons still provided unrivalled status and prestige because of real geostrategic clout.

Israel

Israel's nuclear weapons programme is believed to have begun during the Cold War and it is worth mentioning it here as it sits apart from other the nuclear weapons states. Israel has never declared that it has nuclear weapons and has officially adopted a policy of ambiguity towards them. It is, however, universally acknowledged that Israel possesses its own nuclear weapons capability. Israel's programme is believed to have started after the Suez Crisis in 1956. In July 1956, the Egyptian government, under the leadership of Gamal Abdel Nasser, nationalized the Suez Canal. The canal provides a crucial navigation route through Europe to Africa and it had been controlled by the UK and France. Egypt's nationalization of the canal meant that it owned and operated this essential trading route.

Israel, the UK and France formed a joint plan to invade Egypt. Israeli forces attacked the Sinai Peninsula on 29 October 1956. UK and French troops landed in Port Said and Port Faud, occupying the Canal Zone a few days later. While Israel achieved military success, the operation failed due to diplomatic intervention from the US, Soviet Union and UN, forcing a ceasefire. Israel's strategic vulnerability in the region was evident after the crisis. It confirmed to Israeli leaders that they could not rely on support from external states to ensure security and survival. Julian Borger, writing in the *Guardian* in 2014, argued that France supplied nuclear materials and technical support to Israel due to 'a sense of guilt over letting Israel down in the 1956 conflict, sympathy from French-Jewish scientists, intelligence sharing over Algeria and a drive to sell French expertise abroad'.[13]

Israel established a heavy water moderated reactor, which is needed for a nuclear reactor to slow down the neutrons produced during the fission reaction so that the chain reaction can be sustained. It has been suggested that Israel conducted a successful nuclear explosion on the eve of the Six-Day War in 1967; however, it is hard to find evidence that the test occurred. The *New York Times* published a piece in 2017 reporting that:

> On the eve of the Arab-Israeli war ... Israeli officials raced to assemble an atomic device and developed a plan to detonate it atop a mountain in the Sinai Peninsula as a warning to Egyptian and other Arab forces. ... The secret contingency plan, called a 'doomsday operation' by Itzhak Yaakov, [a retired brigadier general] would have been invoked if Israel feared it was going to lose the 1967 conflict. The demonstration blast, Israeli officials believed, would intimidate Egypt and surrounding Arab states – Syria, Iraq and Jordan – into backing off. Israel won the war so quickly that the atomic device was never moved to Sinai.[14]

Israel has neither confirmed nor denied this strategy.

Israel is believed to have conducted an undeclared nuclear test in 1979, referred to as the Vela incident, in which an unidentified flash of light was detected by an American Vela satellite near the South African territory of Prince Edward Islands in the Indian Ocean.

This was thought to be an undeclared joint nuclear test carried out by Israel and South Africa.

It is generally considered that Israel conducted a successful nuclear weapons test again in 1987, working with South Africa. In July 1987, the *International Defense Review* reported that in May 1987, Israel had successfully test fired a nuclear weapon delivery system, by test firing an intermediate range ballistic missile capable of carrying a nuclear warhead. The missile, named Jericho II, travelled 500 miles.[15] Israel maintains the policy position that it 'will not be the first to introduce nuclear weapons into the Middle East'.[16] It is not clear if this means the first to have these weapons, or whether this would indicate that to Israel nuclear weapons would only be used as a last resort option, as a massive retaliation with nuclear weapons against a country whose military has invaded and/or destroyed much of the country. Despite its policy of ambiguity, in January 2025 it was estimated that Israel has 90 nuclear warheads.[17]

Iraq

Saddam Hussein, the president of Iraq (1979–2003), chairman of the Revolutionary Guard and prime minister, ruled through a brutal regime of internal oppression of opposition and established a personality cult. He declared his intention to develop nuclear weapons, and use the retaliatory deterrent power to counter any response from Israel. Once Iraq had acquired nuclear weapons, Saddam planned to fight a 'patient war – a war of attrition that would reclaim Arab lands lost in the 1967 Six Day War'. (In 1967, Israel had captured the Sinai, Gaza, West Bank, East Jerusalem and the Golan Heights.) This, Saddam believed, would enable him to become the 'hero' of the Arab world.[18]

Iraq's nuclear programme had commenced in the late 1950s with the purchase of a Soviet-made research reactor. The programme lagged for many years due to political instability, but took off again in 1973, when Saddam Hussein became head of the Iraqi Atomic Energy Committee. Iraq evaded IAEA weapons inspectors for years. Saddam worked with scientists and formed agreements with France, Brazil, India, Italy and the Soviet Union. He acquired a 40-megawatt research reactor along with 93 per cent highly enriched uranium. By the early 1980s Iraq was 'reportedly within a few years of being able to manufacture a simple nuclear device'.[19]

Iraq had fought an eight-year war with Iran from 1980 to 1988, during which Iraq used chemical weapons against Iranian troops and Kurdish insurgents. Iraqi accounts state that they used '19,500 chemical bombs, over 54,000 chemical artillery shells and over 27,000 short range chemical filled rockets from 1983–1988'.[20]

On 2 August 1990, Iraqi forces invaded Kuwait, which Saddam believed was an integral part of Iraq. Figures for Iraq's debt to Kuwait prior to the invasion vary from US$14 billion to the lower value of US$8–10 billion. The loans were to fund the Iran–Iraq War, a debt which Kuwait had refused to forgive. Many believe that oil was the primary reason for the invasion; after invading Kuwait, Saddam controlled 20 per cent of the world's oil reserves.[21]

The US response to the invasion was swift. George H.W. Bush met with the British Prime Minister Margaret Thatcher the following day and they issued a joint press conference condemning Saddam's actions. On 5 August 1990, Saudi Arabia gave consent to station US troops there.

Iraqi forces quickly asserted control of Kuwait, and the Kuwaiti leadership fled to Saudi Arabia. On 28 August 1990 Saddam declared Kuwait a province of Iraq. Saddam's actions marked the first major crisis of the new global era.

In November 1990 the UN Security Council issued Resolution 678, calling on Iraq to withdraw all of its forces from Kuwait by 15 January 1991. Saddam refused to do so and, on 17 January 1991, Operation Desert Storm, a coalition of forces from 35 states, began with an air campaign, followed by a land campaign on 24 February 1991. The land campaign lasted 100 hours, ending on 28 February 1991 when coalition forces liberated Kuwait and advanced into Iraq territory.

In April 1991, UN Security Council Resolution 687 required Iraq to declare, destroy or render harmless its WMD arsenal and production infrastructure. This resolution also demanded that Iraq forego all future development and acquisition of WMDs.

The Gulf War and subsequent sanctions all but destroyed Iraq's nuclear programme and it is thought that the regime 'made no attempt to acquire nuclear weapons between 1991 and 2003'.[22]

The remit and jurisdiction of future IAEA weapons inspections changed as a result of the case of Iraq. In 1997 the IAEA declared an additional protocol which enables inspectors to enter and inspect undeclared sites.

India and Pakistan

In the post-Cold War period, both India and Pakistan worked to develop their own nuclear weapons capability. Academics have argued that any use of these weapons would be contained within a regional territorial dispute between the two powers. For both states, nuclear weapons are associated with survival and power. Both states share borders with China, a nuclear neighbour. Since the Partition of British India, India and Pakistan have fought several wars, in 1947, 1965, 1971 and 1999.

When India gained independence, it chose to pursue a foreign policy stance of non-alignment, in a move to maintain autonomy over its security decision-making. Over the decades, this policy has evolved. Throughout the Cold War, India had received support from the Soviet Union. During the 1965 war between India and Pakistan, the Soviet Union played a mediating role and it used its veto power half a dozen times between 1957 and 1971.

> The Soviet Union supported India during the Cold War, notably during the 1971 war between India and Pakistan, in which the US and China sided with Pakistan. This was

arguably the peak of the Indo–Soviet relationship and also the year that the two countries signed a treaty of friendship and cooperation.[23]

India had launched a nuclear test in 1974,[24] the 'Smiling Buddha', claiming it was pursuing the peaceful use of nuclear energy and it had no intention of developing nuclear weapons.[25] But on 11 May 1998, India successfully test-fired its own nuclear weapon. Its justification for the development of such a programme was strategic concerns about the power and policy choices of neighbouring China and Pakistan. India no longer had support from the Soviet Union. Developing a nuclear capability was a way to secure its position among hostile neighbours.

India has always maintained that its nuclear weapons are purely defensive, to be used as a last resort: 'Our nuclear weapons are meant purely as a deterrent against nuclear adventure by an adversary.'[26] Indian nuclear weapons have been named after religious mythological characters, indicating a link to its cultural independence and history. Indian long-range intercontinental missiles were named after mythological characters from the *Bhagavad Gita*, the Hindu sacred text. The first missile of the programme was named Prithvi after Maharaja Prithviraj Chauhan, who defended the kingdom against Muslim invader Shahab-ud-din Ghauri. More aggressive symbolism is connected to the Agni-Prime (2021), a surface-to-surface medium range missile; the 'Agni' refers to the Hindu god of fire. The name Agni emphasizes the destructive nature of these weapons.[27]

Similar to India, Pakistani scientists started working on a nuclear weapons programme in the early 1970s, though this only came to fruition in 1998. Pakistan has argued that it needs nuclear weapons to deter India. After it conducted five nuclear tests in 1998, Prime Minister Nawaz Sharif gave an address to the nation in which he stated:

> Today, God the great has bestowed us the courage and determination to enable us to make a decision to take a decisive step, which has become inevitable for the sake of our country's security. ... India is running so far ahead in the nuclear arms race that there is no option but to stop it. A retaliatory action has become indispensable for the sake of peace and security of this region.[28]

In the history of antagonism between India and Pakistan, nuclear weapons have limited conflict. By 1999, both had acquired nuclear weapons and the Kashmir region remained a long-standing cause of tension. They had gone to war over it in 1947, 1965 and 1971. But in 1999, when India and Pakistan fought the Kargil War, it lasted just two months. A contributing factor to abbreviating the war was that both sides had nuclear weapons.

So while there was optimism among advocates of non-proliferation that nuclear weapons were no longer useful weapons of war, in the decade after the end of the Cold War, they were proved wrong. To a handful of states, nuclear weapons have still been seen as important weapons to balance power and ensure security and stability. The strategic value of these weapons has outweighed any moral or political arguments.

This chapter has shown that the end of the Cold War led to initial optimism that the liberal democracies had prevailed, leading to a more peaceful world. This was sadly not the case. Conflict still continued and nuclear weapons were still desirable for some states. What was seen in this period was a greater role for the UN and a greater focus upon the welfare of the people within conflict, the victims of war. The challenge for the future was to ensure that this perception advanced.

7
9/11 AND THE NUCLEAR THREAT

At 08:46 (ET) on 11 September 2001, Al-Qaeda terrorists flew a domestic airliner into one of the Twin Towers of the World Trade Center in New York City. A second plane crashed into the other tower 16 minutes later. Both towers collapsed shortly after. Within the next hour, a third airliner collided into the Pentagon and a fourth crash-landed in a field in Pennsylvania; it had been heading towards the Capitol Building. The 19 terrorists who orchestrated the 9/11 attacks 'willingly and wantonly killed themselves, the passengers, and crews of the four aircraft they commandeered and the approximately 3,000 people working at or visiting both the World Trade Center and the Pentagon'.[1] The events of that day signified a changed world.

9/11 proved mass destruction could be caused without possessing advanced technology; the terrorists used box-cutters and domestic airliners to create terror, turning planes into weapons. The Twin Towers symbolized Western capitalism and US hegemony, the focus of global activity for the modern world. What were nuclear weapons for in a post-9/11 world? How could the nuclear threat be addressed in this new environment?

9/11 was a wake-up call: '[T]he enormity and sheer scale of the simultaneous suicide attacks on September 11 eclipsed anything previously seen in terrorism.'[2] This time the conflict did not emerge directly from states, but from the militant groups, working as a global network of terror. Terrorism was not new, the US National Security Strategy (1996) had long since identified terrorism as a continuing threat, however what was new was the scale and coordination of the 9/11 attacks. Their planning was organized and sophisticated, they entered into the US undetected, and obtained visas to do so, they took flight lessons *within* the US prior to their attacks. How could this type of threat be deterred? The 9/11 attacks meant that previous assessments of global security needed to change. 9/11 highlighted that in addition to state actors, non-state actors, individuals or groups of individuals not affiliated or funded by the state but able to exercise significant influence, posed an international security threat.

While the scale and reach of the threats facing the world increased and the actors conducting these threats varied, the international response to the terror attacks targeted states as the main sponsors of terrorism. This led to the 'War on Terror' and war in Afghanistan (2001–21). In this changed environment, the nuclear threat continued to be politicized. The association of nuclear weapons with that of chemical and biological weapons was once again bought to the fore and strengthened. The term 'WMD' began to be used within the media more and more frequently, and Saddam's Hussein's threats to acquire and use these weapons provided the rationale for war in Iraq (2003).

Post-9/11, the threat of nuclear proliferation continued; a small number of states still sought to develop these weapons.

On 29 January 2002, in his State of the Union Address, US President George W. Bush spoke about the threat to security posed by an 'Axis of Evil', by which he meant Iraq, North Korea and Iran. Iran was seen as a sponsor of terrorism, supporting groups such as Hezbollah in Lebanon and Hamas in the Palestinian territories. In addition, the US voiced alarm that Iran was developing nuclear weapons which would destabilize the Middle East region and threaten US interests and allies. North Korea's nuclear ambitions were also the subject of Bush's speech. Despite becoming a party to the NPT in 1985, North Korea would leave the NPT in 2003, declaring that it faced existential threats from the US and South Korea. North Korea is the first and only state to have done this. Despite attempts to mediate with North Korea to stop the development of its nuclear programme, in 2006 it successfully tested a nuclear weapon.

9/11 AND THE NUCLEAR THREAT

The picture is not all gloomy. Ironically, 9/11 and the threat that non-state actors could acquire nuclear weapons created a new impetus for arms control and disarmament, as it forced advocates of arms control to consider new strategies to limit the spread of nuclear weapons. The work of the NPT had, for several years before 9/11, focused on addressing horizontal and vertical proliferation. After 9/11 its members recognized that they also now needed to devise collective measures to prevent non-state actors from acquiring nuclear materials. This called for new monitoring mechanisms.

Increased political and public debate and protests about the rationale for the 2003 Iraq War and the ethical objections to this war served to reignite debates about the morality of nuclear weapons. President Obama, in 2009, called for a world free of nuclear weapons: 'To put an end to Cold War thinking, we will reduce the role of nuclear weapons in our national security strategy, and urge others to do the same.'[3]

Reaction to the Iraq War and the progress achieved by the Obama administration to spotlight arms control and disarmament strengthened the anti-nuclear movement. In 2017, the Treaty on the Prohibition of Nuclear Weapons was declared and entered into force four years later. Though it did not include nuclear states, this was the first agreement to call for a total ban of nuclear weapons.

Nuclear terrorism and the spread of nuclear materials

The consequences of 9/11 for the nuclear threat was that it was now framed in connection to the War on Terror and referred to as part of the wider threat from WMDs. The term WMD became an integral part of American security discourse.

George W. Bush's rationale for the war was to safeguard against the threat of Iraq's WMDs and end Saddam's support of terrorist organizations.

The decision to go to war was highly controversial, in the absence of secure evidence that Saddam had WMDs or that Iraq had links to Al-Qaeda. UN Secretary General Kofi Annan made clear that the war was not sanctioned by the UN Security Council or in accordance with the UN's founding charter. The US and UK positions rejected this. UK Prime Minister Tony Blair said that Saddam was in breach of UN Resolutions calling for Iraq to give up its supply of WMDs.[4] Saddam had attacked the Kurdish population with chemical weapons in the 1980s; if he could sanction the use of chemical weapons, might he do the same with nuclear weapons?

The war sparked massive protests throughout the world. On 15 February 2003, millions of people across 600 cities worldwide protested. Anti-war organizers claimed that the worldwide demonstrations formed the largest peace protest since the Vietnam War. The war is believed to have cost the US a total of US$2 trillion. The US Department of Defense estimated that the American death toll of the war was 4,431.

The estimated death toll of Iraqis ranges across studies, with a 2013 assessment placing the toll for the duration of US occupation at approximately half a million as a result of war-related causes. Millions more Iraqis were displaced.[5]

Investigations discovered found no evidence that Iraq was manufacturing WMDs and Iraq was years away from acquiring any kind of nuclear capacity.[6] These findings were backed up by the 9/11 Commission report in 2004, which found no evidence that Iraq was working with Al-Qaeda.

After 9/11, world leaders argued that non-state actors might acquire nuclear materials and use these in acts of terrorism, leading to an even larger attack than that of 9/11.[7] Nuclear materials could be adapted to create radiological dispersion devices (dirty bombs). These are not technically nuclear weapons, since conventional explosives are used to disseminate radiological material. However, the threat of the spread of nuclear materials, and the terror that such a weapon could cause in a metropolitan area, was enough to trigger international action. In 2004, the UN Security Council passed Resolution 1540, which declared that: 'All States shall refrain from providing any form of support to non-state actors that attempt to develop, acquire, manufacture, possess, transport, transfer or use nuclear, chemical and biological weapons and their means of delivery, in particular for terrorist purposes.'[8] The resolution reflected a broader understanding of the threat posed by nuclear weapons. Previous assessments of potential use of nuclear weapons had focused on this use at a strategic level in the form of large-scale conflict between two global powers with knowable rules of engagement. This meant that it was possible to predict threats and promote and pursue diplomatic solutions. Post-9/11, greater attention had to be paid to the limits of what could be known. Donald Rumsfeld famously stated at a press conference in 2002 that, while there are things we know, 'we also know there are known unknowns – that is to say, we know there are some things we do not know. But there are also *unknown unknowns*, the ones we don't know we didn't know'.[9] Nuclear materials had now entered the category of known – and therefore worrying – unknowns.

Nuclear weapons still desirable to some ...

Alongside the possibility that non-state actors could acquire and use nuclear materials, the threat that hostile states might still try to develop nuclear weapons remained. Nuclear weapons were still strategically desirable weapons.

Iran

Iran's nuclear programme began under Mohammad Reza Shah's rule in 1957; the US and Iran agreed to the Agreement for Co-operation Concerning Civil Uses of Atomic Energy in 1957 through the Atoms for Peace programme, whereby the US would assist Iran to develop the peaceful uses of atomic energy for humanitarian purposes. Two years later, the Shah established the

Tehran Nuclear Research Centre to work with the US to further develop nuclear materials and technology. In 1967, the US supplied Iran with a five-megawatt nuclear research reactor. Iran ratified the NPT in 1970. The 1979 revolution brought Ayatollah Ruhollah Khomeini to power; he believed that WMDs, including nuclear weapons, were forbidden in Islam.[10] Iran is thought to have restarted its nuclear energy programme in 1989 after Khomeini's death. In the early 2000s Iran refused to suspend its enrichment activities despite demands from the UN Security Council and asserted its right to enrich uranium for peaceful purposes.

In 2002, CNN published photographs of two suspected (but undeclared) nuclear sites in Arak and Natanz. US officials argued that Iran was developing a secret nuclear weapons programme. They asserted that the sites were producing heavy water and enriched uranium. This would make Iran self-sufficient in nuclear fuel, but could also be utilized to produce nuclear weapons. Iranian officials denied any such intentions, claiming that the plants were for experiments with radioactivity. Despite this, the amount of uranium Iran was enriching was alarming to the IAEA weapons inspectors. Sanctions were imposed on Iran and it agreed to more stringent inspections.

Iran has always asserted that its right to acquire nuclear energy, as opposed to weapons, is a demonstration of its independence and right to modernize as a state. Supreme Leader Ali Khamenei stated in 2003, after the US invasion of Iraq: '[W]e don't want a nuclear bomb, we are even opposed to chemical weapons.'[11]

A year later, President Khatami said Iran had a right to acquire nuclear energy, but reiterated that 'Iran won't go for nuclear weapons at all'.[12]

The election of President Mahmoud Ahmadinejad, his angry reaction to sanctions imposed on the country and his statements about the US as the 'Great Satan'[13] elevated the West's concerns. Though he, like his predecessors, maintained that Iran did not seek nuclear weapons.

In 2010, the US Pentagon estimated that 'Iran's nuclear program and its willingness to keep open the possibility of developing nuclear weapons is a central part of its deterrent strategy. ... Iran is developing a range of technical capabilities that could be applied to the production of nuclear weapons if the decision is made to do so'.[14] In that same year, Iran hosted the International Conference on Nuclear Disarmament and Non-Proliferation, at which Ayatollah Ali Khamenei referred to the threat of the use of chemical, biological and nuclear weapons, stating that:

> [T]he Iranian nation, which is itself a victim of the use of chemical weapons, feels more than other nations the danger of the production and accumulation of such weapons and is ready to put all of its resources in the way of dealing with it. We consider the use of these weapons to be *Haram* (forbidden), and the effort to protect mankind from this disaster is everybody's duty.[15]

A breakthrough towards a comprehensive agreement with Iran to limit its nuclear programme came in 2013.

President Hassan Rouhani took office that year and agreed to a Joint Comprehensive Plan of Action – 'the Iran deal' – which froze Iran's nuclear activities in exchange for a lifting of economic sanctions. A larger agreement was reached in 2015 between Iran, the US, UK, France, Russia, China and Germany (P5+1); this imposed strict limits on Iran's nuclear programme for 10–15 years in exchange for a lifting of economic sanctions. In 2018, during Donald Trump's first presidency, the US withdrew from the agreement. The US argued that Iran had gradually breached the agreement's limits, increasing uranium enrichment and stockpiles. Trump said his administration would withdraw from the deal as it had not addressed Iran's regional activities and ballistic missile programme. The other P5 members stated that the deal remained a binding international agreement. Iran's nuclear ambitions continue to be the subject of great concern. Since 2019:

> [I]t has lifted the cap on its stockpile of uranium, which is now 30 times the level permitted; increased its enrichment activities to 60%, significantly beyond the 3.67% permitted under the Joint Comprehensive Plan of Action; expanded its enrichment capabilities and resumed activity at nuclear facilities that were previously prohibited under the terms of the deal.[16]

The US Office of the Director of National Intelligence has concluded that 'while Iran does not appear to be currently pursuing development of a nuclear device, the nuclear activities undertaken since 2020 "better position it to produce a nuclear device, if it chooses to do so" '.[17] In May 2025, the IAEA reported that Iran was enriching uranium to 60 per cent levels. This is far beyond the 3.67 agreed in the Joint Comprehensive Plan of Action. The IAEA reported that 'while enrichment is not forbidden in and of itself, "the fact that Iran is the only non-nuclear-weapon State in the world that is producing and accumulating uranium enriched to 60 per cent remains a matter of serious concern"'.[18]

In response to increasing concerns about Iran's nuclear programme, on 13 June 2025, Israel launched preemptive military strikes against Iran, targeting suspected nuclear facilities and military sites. Iran responded with a series of ballistic missile and drone attacks on Israel. On 22 June, the US bombed military sites in Fordow, Natanz and Isfahan. Iran responded by bombing the US military base in Qatar. Israel and Iran agreed to a US-brokered ceasefire on 23 June, leaving the status of Iran's nuclear programme uncertain.

North Korea

North Korea began its nuclear energy programme in the late 1950s after the Korean War under the leadership of Kim Il Sung. In 1956, North Korea and the Soviet Union signed two agreements to co-operate on nuclear research projects, which enabled North Korean scientists to receive professional training in the fields of nuclear science and technology. Throughout the Cold War, North Korea aligned itself with the

Soviet Union and is one of a few remaining communist states in the world.

Both North and South Korea claim sovereignty over the entire peninsula and fought a bitter war in 1950, ending in an Armistice agreement in 1953. North Korea identifies South Korea as its principal threat and had objected to the stationing of US tactical nuclear weapons there. These were removed in 1991. Diplomatic dialogue has taken place sporadically between both states since the 1970s. The North Asian security specialist Alexandre Mansourov has documented that Kim Il Sung believed:

> In the event of an all-out war, he could not use nuclear weapons against his opponents in the South because he understood that he would never be forgiven by the Korean people should he ever use an atomic weapon against his own brethren, even if they were 'murderous puppets of American imperialism'.[19]

In December 1985, North Korea signed the NPT. Its membership indicated that North Korea appeared to be working with the international community to reduce the nuclear threat. But it did not sign a nuclear safeguards agreement with the IAEA, and therefore did not allow any inspection of its facilities. The IAEA still assisted North Korea with its uranium mining programme.

After the Cold War, the Soviet Union changed its defence policy and recognized South Korea in 1990, establishing formal diplomatic relations, which North

Korea viewed as a betrayal. Kim Il Sung believed that this undermined North Korea's claim to be the sole legitimate government of Korea. He opposed the ideological belief of his neighbours and the close relations they had with the US. Russia's actions also weakened North Korea's leverage as it was no longer Russia's sole ally in the region. As North Korea became increasingly isolated from the rest of the world, a furious DPRK Foreign Ministry released a memorandum stating that Soviet recognition of the ROK 'will leave us no other choice but to take measures to provide ... for ourselves some weapons for which we have so far relied on the alliance'.[20] It had relied heavily on the Soviet Union for trade. The removal of this support led to extreme economic hardship and a decade of famine. Kim Il Sung died in 1994, leaving a power vacuum and a succession struggle. His son, Kim Jong Il, established power after his death and promoted policies of economic reform and military supremacy. In particular, the political philosophy of *Juche* is core to all strategic decision-making. *Juche*, which derives partly from Marxism-Leninism, means 'being the master of revolution and reconstruction in one country. ... Rejecting dependence on others and using one's brains'.[21] The principles of political independence, economic independence and self-reliance in defence are the three characteristics fundamental to *Juche* philosophy, which partly finds expression in its weapons programme. North Korea has always stated that it needs nuclear weapons to deter strategic threats from its neighbours, Japan and

South Korea's Western capitalist ideals and defence agreements with the US.

In 2003, North Korea finally withdrew from the NPT, blaming US aggression. The US, a year earlier, had specifically identified North Korea as posing a global danger to the world, although Kim Jong Il stated that despite withdrawing from the treaty, 'we have no intention of producing nuclear weapons and our nuclear activities at this stage will be confined only to peaceful purposes such as the production of electricity'.[22]

Diplomatic efforts to prevent North Korea from developing its nuclear weapons programme failed, as did harsh economic sanctions. The famine of 1994–8 killed an estimated two to three million people.[23] In October 2006 North Korea successfully test-fired a nuclear weapon, and conducted six subsequent nuclear tests between 2006 and 2017. It declared itself a nuclear weapons state in 2022.

The case of North Korea demonstrates that, despite changes to the West's threat perception post-9/11, nuclear weapons remained important strategic deterrent weapons. To North Korea, as with India and Pakistan, political, historical and ideological interests require strategic stability. Nuclear weapons serve as this tool, assuring prestige, independence and survival.

A world free of nuclear weapons?

All has not been lost for the anti-nuclear movement. The election of Barack Obama in 2008 led to a revision of US foreign policy. Obama, during his presidential campaign, had pledged to end the war in Iraq, rebuild and construct alliances and secure, destroy and stop the spread of WMDs. The campaign team viewed the policies of the Bush administration as outdated, and out of step with an increasingly globalized, interconnected world. The security of the American people, Obama asserted, is 'inextricably linked to the security of all people', noting:

> We know that these are not the best of times for America's reputation in the world. We know that the War in Iraq has cost us in lives and treasure, in influence and respect. We have seen the consequences of a foreign policy based on a flawed ideology, and a belief that tough talk can replace real strength and vision.[24]

To restore its reputation, the US needs to promote international cooperation and multilateralism: 'Whether it's global terrorism or pandemic disease, dramatic climate change or the proliferation of weapons of mass annihilation, the threats we face at the dawn of the 21st century can no longer be contained by borders and boundaries.'[25]

To advocates of nuclear non-proliferation, the Iraq War violated all their core principles. The Bush administration bypassed the mechanisms of arms control and used force to attack Iraq, alleging the presence of WMDs. The war in Iraq 'set a perilous precedent and a flawed formula for dealing with other global proliferation challenges'.[26] Many policy

9/11 AND THE NUCLEAR THREAT

Figure 7.1: Estimated global nuclear warhead inventories, 2025

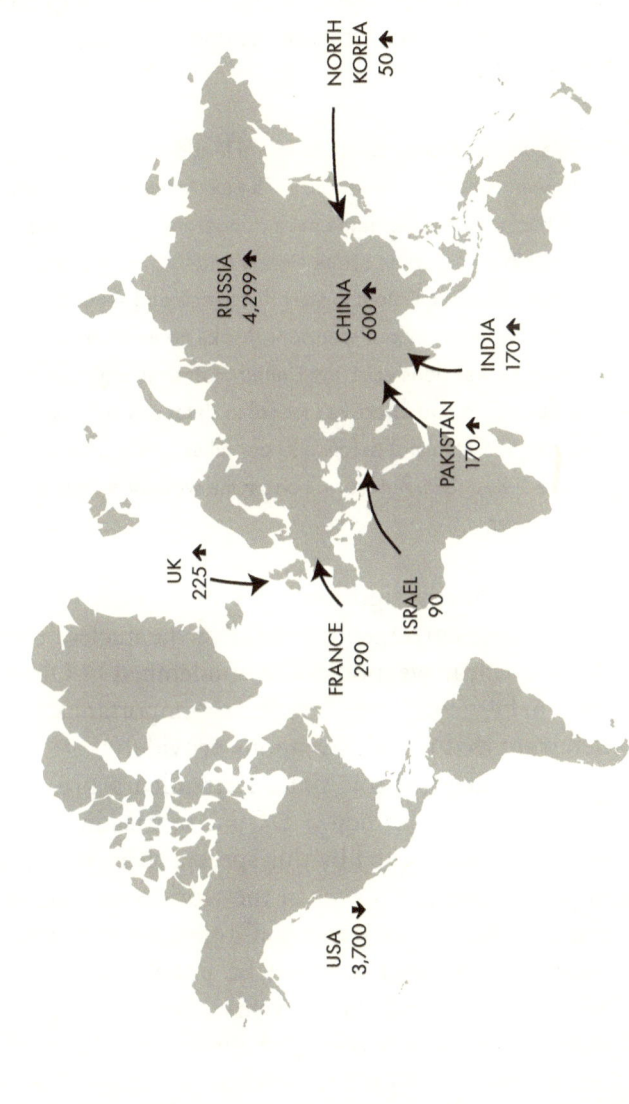

makers in the Obama administration shared this view and sought to reinvigorate past efforts to implement a nuclear non-proliferation regime. On 5 April 2009, Obama declared in Prague:

> We are here today because moral leadership is more powerful than any weapon. ... The existence of thousands of nuclear weapons is the most dangerous legacy of the Cold War. ... Today, I state clearly and with conviction America's commitment to seek the peace and security of a world without nuclear weapons. Make no mistake: As long as these weapons exist, the United States will maintain a safe, secure and effective arsenal to deter any adversary, and guarantee that defence to our allies – including the Czech Republic. But we will begin the work of reducing our arsenal.[27]

These remarks signified this new push to create multilateral agreements to address the nuclear threat. While nuclear weapons were condemned in Obama's speech, his remarks still stressed the important strategic deterrent that nuclear weapons provide.

As a student at this time, I attended a prestigious conference in Washington, DC and saw leading experts enthused and excited by this speech: there was finally hope. The largest power in the world was discussing the possibility that states could give up their nuclear weapons, and that it might be possible to live in a nuclear-free world. In the years after this, there was increased progress to establish international consensus and agreement to limit the spread of nuclear weapons.

One of the concrete steps in this vision was to form further agreements to ban nuclear testing. During his 2009 Nobel Peace Prize speech, Obama spoke about working towards a Comprehensive Test Ban Treaty (CTBT). The Partial Test Ban Treaty had been signed in 1963 (see Chapter 5), banning any nuclear explosion in the atmosphere, outer space or under water – but not underground. The CTBT would have banned *all* nuclear explosions. A CTBT resolution was re-sent to the UN General Assembly in 1996, where it was met with overall support. However, the Treaty could not come into force without ratification from China, Egypt, Iran, Israel, Russia and the US. Obama sought to gain US ratification of the Treaty and attempted to present a CTBT proposal to the Senate in 2010, but once again this failed to obtain ratification.

The US and Russia signed the Strategic Arms Reduction Treaty (referred to as the New START Treaty) on 8 April 2010, and this has been extended to 2026. It reduces US and Russian deployed strategic warheads by approximately one third and missile and bomber launchers by half. The treaty contained strong verification mechanisms, which included site inspections, data exchanges and notifications about the movement of strategic systems. The treaty did not limit the number of operationally inactive warheads stockpiled by each side. This was important as each side had thousands.

In 1995 and 2007 attempts failed to reinvigorate the Fissile Material Cut-Off Treaty and make it a legally binding treaty banning the production of fissile material for nuclear weapons and other nuclear explosive devices. Non-nuclear weapon states, as members of the NPT, are already prohibited from acquiring fissile material for weapons. The proposed treaty would have imposed restrictions on all nine of the world's nuclear weapon states. Attempts continued and, on 7 May 2015, a Group of Governmental Experts submitted a proposal to the UN General Assembly for a Treaty. In 2016 the UN General Assembly adopted Resolution 71/259 to establish a 'high level fissile material cut off treaty (FMTC) expert preparatory group to recommend the most effective route to establish a FMTC'. Despite further efforts to reach an agreement, no treaty has yet been signed. Objections to the treaty once again centred on verification measures; it was hard to design a regime that satisfied all parties. Nuclear states were concerned that any treaty would weaken their own security and limit nuclear weapon deterrent capabilities.

The threat of the spread of nuclear materials was also promoted by the Obama administration. They held a series of high-level security summits in 2010, 2012, 2014 and 2016 to foster international cooperation to tackle the threat of international nuclear terrorism and to monitor the spread of nuclear materials.

The environmental threat

A nuclear accident in Fukushima continued to stoke public anxiety about the safety of civil nuclear energy plants. In March 2011, Japan suffered a devastating earthquake measuring 9.0 on the Richter scale, which triggered a tsunami, killing 19,500 people.[28] Japan's nuclear power plant in Fukushima was engulfed by waves, which caused a massive disaster. Radioactive fuel leaked from three of the reactors. The quick actions of the experts at the plant reduced the impact and it is estimated that the long-term risks of exposure from the accident are low. Despite this, an exclusion zone remains around the area of Fukushima and work is still required to keep it safe. This event serves as a reminder of the dangers associated with civil nuclear power.

The public and political condemnation of the Iraq War and political advances to extend the arms control regime emboldened the disarmament movement, leading to a greater calls for international action against nuclear weapons. The campaign adopted a new stance, highlighting the rights of individuals and human security. Non-governmental organizations (NGOs), voluntary organizations and community groups addressed the catastrophic, indiscriminate consequences of nuclear use and testing. They argued that the very existence of nuclear weapons presents a global security threat. This campaign approach was not new, as we saw in previous chapters: it was the basis for many of the protests throughout the Cold War. What was new was *how* this argument was put across in campaigning. The International Campaign to Abolish Nuclear Weapons movement spearheaded the protests; this is a global movement of over 100 NGOs, working to mobilize 'civil society around the world to support the specific objective of prohibiting and eliminating nuclear weapons'.[29]

The International Campaign to Abolish Nuclear Weapons movement was inspired by the success of the Campaign to Ban Landmines, the Ottawa Convention (1997) and landmine ban. Working with a number of NGOs, International Physicians for the Prevention of Nuclear War, the Women's International League for Peace and Freedom and the Campaign for Nuclear Disarmament,[30] which had been established to promote nuclear disarmament, they developed the Humanitarian Initiative. This called for a complete ban of nuclear weapons, drawing on the anti-nuclear campaigns of the Cold War to refocus international attention to their cause. The campaign sought to force nuclear weapons states to prove how they could possess such weapons, promote the norms of human rights and freedom and be members of the international community, while also maintaining weapons capability that, if used, would cause such devastation. This campaign built international momentum among non-nuclear weapon states, though it failed to persuade states allied with nuclear-armed states.

The Humanitarian Initiative was addressed at the 2010 NPT review conference (Revcon), where members expressed 'their deep concern at the catastrophic humanitarian consequences of any use of nuclear weapons'.[31] Following this, there were Preparatory Committee Meetings in Norway, Mexico and Austria between 2013 and 2014, focused on the humanitarian effects of nuclear detonations. The Humanitarian Initiative quickly gathered praise from NGOs and non-nuclear weapon states, such as Norway, Austria, Switzerland and Brazil.

By the time that the NPT review conference was held in 2015, 160 states had endorsed the Humanitarian Initiative, but the conference failed to endorse a consensus final document. An open-ended working group was established in the UN General Assembly to look at ways of taking forward the disarmament agenda, which led to calls for a nuclear weapons ban treaty. In December 2016, the UN General Assembly adopted a resolution calling for the 'launch of negotiations on a legally binding instrument to prohibit nuclear weapons'.[32] On 7 July 2017, 122 non-nuclear weapons states voted to adopt the Treaty on the Prohibition of Nuclear Weapons. In doing so, they agreed to the prohibition of the possession, use and threat of use of nuclear weapons. Nuclear weapon states and their allies refused to sign. They argued that it was irrelevant, as only non-nuclear states could be compliant with its obligations.

Where the treaty and the debates throughout the past two decades are of importance is in reinforcing the nuclear stigma. Globalization has increased awareness of the devastating effects of nuclear weapons. Increased communication and information have meant that this campaign has reignited public protest. The focus is on the weapons themselves and the devastation that they cause, empowering a much broader community to debate the nuclear threat.

8
CONCLUSION

In this final chapter I want to look at the role of nuclear weapons today, focusing on the central themes of this book to highlight the strategic, political and moral significance of these weapons. In 2025, the Russia–Ukraine War is a reminder that the strategic deterrent quality of nuclear weapons remains of great significance. Russia, throughout the war, has drawn attention to its nuclear capability, both through threatening rhetoric and in military exercises and demonstrations. In doing so, it has reminded the world of the massive strategic advantage that it has. Transfer operations commenced in 2023 to station nuclear weapons in Belarus, a neighbour to Ukraine. Russia has warned states that any direct support for Ukraine will result in economic or military retaliation. In the same year, it amended its nuclear doctrine to state that it 'is prepared to use nuclear weapons in retaliation to nuclear attacks, as well as conventional attacks that threaten the sovereignty or territorial integrity of Russia or Belarus'.[1] To date, NATO member states have supplied arms and ammunition to Ukraine, but not committed boots on the ground.

We live in a world with a broad range of security threats, involving a broad range of actors. 'Grey zone warfare' is a salient 21st-century phenomenon: this is conflict below the threshold of all-out war but no longer within the realms of peace. Examples include cyber-attacks, attacks on the undersea electricity cables that supply global access to the internet, targeted assassination and misinformation campaigns. Modern conflict, such as the Russia–Ukraine War, constitutes a new type of warfare involving grey zone strategies as well as conventional methods. Meanwhile, conventional forms of warfare are also advancing, turning scientific advances in artificial intelligence to military use, for example, and devising ever more deadly drone technology.

Since the end of the Cold War, despite the US, UK, France and Russia having reduced their stockpiles of nuclear weapons, we are now seeing a trend towards nuclear modernization. Nuclear weapons themselves are changing; the programmes of the nuclear powers have created smaller nuclear weapons, able to be deployed more easily in differing conflict scenarios. There remains the possibility that more states will acquire nuclear weapons and Iran's nuclear energy programme is still a cause of anxiety for the international community.

Politically and diplomatically, the use of nuclear weapons remain taboo. The re-election of Donald Trump in 2024 and the Trump administration's policy of *peace through strength* shows signs of unsettling many established Western norms of statecraft. Indicating that the nuclear taboo might be less firmly entrenched than had been thought.

Russia-Ukraine War

On 24 February 2022, Russia launched dozens of missiles on Ukraine's main cities, backed up by a ground invasion advancing on the capital, Kyiv. Ukraine has resisted, and as it has done so, Russia has increasingly warned that any international involvement to defend Ukraine would have severe consequences. On the day of the invasion, Putin issued a veiled nuclear threat: '[N]o matter who tries to stand in our way or all the more so create threats from our country and our people, they must know that Russia will respond immediately, and the consequences will be such as you have never seen in your entire history.'[2]

Between launching its invasion and July 2023, Russia threatened the use of nuclear weapons 200 times.[3] In September 2024, it amended its Nuclear Principles to 'consider an attack from a non-nuclear state that was backed by a nuclear-armed one to be a "joint attack" in what could be construed as a threat to use nuclear weapons in the war in Ukraine. In such instance, Russia would use nuclear weapons'.[4] This indicates that Russia is increasingly relying on the strategic and political power of nuclear weapons to provide security and immunity for its actions in Ukraine. To some extent this has worked. The US is threatening to pull back from NATO, Ukraine is not a member of NATO and at the time of writing looks very unlikely to become one, and NATO forces have not deployed troops to Ukraine.

Is it still all about nukes?

Scientific innovation has led to technological developments in the conventional sphere. The world has changed considerably since 1945. 2025 includes new domains of warfare, cyber, space and artificial intelligence. We also have weapons capable of creating large-scale 'strategic' destruction, indicating a 'third nuclear age' where these weapons can cause mass harm. Weapons such as hypersonic missiles, capable of travelling well above the speed of sound, autonomous weapons such as drones which do not require humans to control them (colloquially known as 'killer robots') and nanotechnology. These all sound like the products of science fiction, but are the reality of today.

Cybersecurity threats are also extremely prominent on the threat landscape. The cyber domain is fundamental to modern society, so attacks on a country's national infrastructure, targeting power grid systems, water and traffic and the logistical systems could have potentially catastrophic consequences, in some ways comparable to that of a nuclear attack.[5]

Satellite technology systems in space control basic functions of society. These include everything from accessing fuel pumps and making bank transfers to running surveillance systems and logistical support.

Space weather events or an attack on these electronic and satellite systems would have devastating consequences. An electromagnetic pulse (EMP), caused by space weather, or deliberately created as a result of a weapon attack, is an increasing threat. An EMP could be caused by a severe weather event such as a solar storm or by a nuclear weapon detonating high in the earth's atmosphere. Such an explosion would create a pressure wave that would knock out all electronic devices and satellite and communications systems. EMPs do not need to be nuclear; they can also be caused by conventional weapons known as E-Bombs.[6] Reactions to these weapons vary from extreme fear that such an attack would lead to all-out destruction, to observations that the effect would be limited. Any such scenario would still create severe disruption.

The development of advanced forms of 'conventional' warfare then raises the question as to whether or not the nuclear weapons will, in time, become obsolete.

The political future: deterrence and a new nuclear age?

It is hard to argue that the threat posed by nuclear weapons in 2025 is any less serious than it has been in the past. In January 2022, all five declared nuclear weapon states and permanent members of the UN (P5), issued a statement condemning the proliferation of nuclear weapons:

CONCLUSION

> A nuclear war cannot be won and must never be fought. As nuclear use would have far-reaching consequences, we also affirm that nuclear weapons – for as long as they continue to exist – should serve defensive purposes, deter aggression and prevent war. We believe strongly that *the further spread of such weapons must be prevented.* (emphasis my own)[7]

All of the nuclear P5 states, with the exception of China, had, prior to this, declared their commitment to reduce their nuclear forces. The Stockholm International Peace Research Institute's director, Dan Smith, has noted that 'while the total number of nuclear warheads continue to fall as cold war era weapons are gradually dismantled, regrettably we continue to see year on year increases in the number of operational nuclear warheads'.[8]

Since the end of the Cold War, all US administrations have reduced the percentage of US nuclear warheads. This refers to a percentage decrease based on the number of nuclear warheads in a country's arsenal over time. George W. Bush reduced the number by 50 per cent. His father George H.W. Bush reduced this number by 40 per cent, Bill Clinton by 23 per cent.[9] Seeking to encourage greater transparency and promote great discussion of nuclear weapons, the Obama administration in 2010 released declassified information revealing that the US had a stockpile of 5,113 warheads. Gathering a clear picture of nuclear reductions can be confusing as, while old systems are being decommissioned, at the same time the US is updating its nuclear warhead programme. This began in 2010 under President Obama. Since 2010, the US has gradually been reducing its weapons stockpile and decommissioning old weapons systems. The pace of this has been slow. In 2025 the Federation of American Scientists estimated the US had 3,700 nuclear warheads and had retired 1,577.[10]

Successive UK governments have declared their commitment to reduce the UK's nuclear arsenal. From 1974 to 1981, the UK stockpile included approximately 500 warheads.[11] The UK has a single weapons system, the Trident submarine system, and the smallest nuclear arsenal of the P5 nuclear weapon states. The 1998 Strategic Review committed to a reduction in operational warheads to 200. In 2010 the government officially confirmed that the UK had 225 warheads and the 2010 Strategic Defence and Security Review set out a policy of the overall nuclear weapons stockpile to 'no more than 180, this would take effect over the next few years'.[12] The 2015 Strategic Defence Review reaffirmed this. In 2017, The UK House of Commons voted to replace the UK's Vanguard fleet of four submarines carrying Trident nuclear weapons.

Since signing the New START Treaty, Russia has slowly decreased its nuclear warhead stockpile. Russia met the ceiling of 1,550 deployed nuclear warheads mandated by START in 2012. In 2013 this reduced to 1,400. The overall size of Russia's strategic force has fallen due to the replacement of old systems. However, Russia's strategic modernization is motivated by 'maintaining rough overall parity with the United

States, improving weapons survivability and efficiency and national prestige'.[13] In 2025, Russia is estimated to have 4,299 warheads, the world's largest number. This is in addition to 1,150 which are to be retired.[14]

France has the fourth largest nuclear arsenal. It has also steadily reduced its nuclear stockpile and is estimated to have 290 nuclear warheads, down from 300 in 2015. This number has remained stable over the last few decades.

Counting the number of warheads in the stockpile of nuclear weapon states is just one way of measuring states' commitment to reduce their nuclear weapons. It is also important to note the power and range of new weapons systems being developed, as well as the actions and rhetoric of these states.

Despite all of this progress, all five P5 states have shifted their policy over roughly the last decade to declare their intention to update their nuclear weapons capability. Indeed, India[15] and Pakistan[16] are also pursuing this process. This has created a paradoxical situation in which P5 nuclear weapon states are presenting the impression of working to reduce their nuclear weapons stockpile, in accordance with the provisions of the NPT, yet strategic concerns have now dominated and overridden this policy.

Nuclear modernization programmes have involved the development of new delivery systems, improving warhead technology, upgrading command and control systems, and maintaining existing systems. In addition, states are developing smaller, low-yield nuclear weapons, designed to be used in a localized

Figure 8.1: Nuclear intercontinental ballistic missiles, Victory Day parade, Moscow, 2024

conflict environment, principally on the battlefield. The development of such weapons challenges conventional assumptions about Mutually Assured Destruction. Russia began developing low-yield weapons in 2018. The US started in early 2000s. The first Trump administration, in the 2018 Nuclear Posture Review, predicted the possibility that Russia may launch a conventional war in Europe and would be tempted to use such weapons to win. In this situation, a response with high-yield weapons would not seem credible. A better deterrence was to develop similar weapons to deter on a similar scale. For this reason the US has continued to develop a low-yield weapons capability.

China is the only P5 state not to have reduced its nuclear forces. The Federation of American Scientists estimates that China has 600 nuclear warheads and the fastest-growing nuclear arsenal among the nine nuclear armed states. China is predicted to be 'fielding more types and greater numbers of nuclear weapons than ever before', developing its intercontinental ballistic missile capability. China has been refitting its ballistic missile submarines with longer range submarine-launched ballistic missiles. The Pentagon estimates that China's arsenal will surpass 1,000 warheads by 2030.[17]

China's motivation for altering its nuclear posture and modernizing its weapons programme is due to domestic and foreign policy concerns. In particular, China's Paramount Leader, Xi Jinping, in 2023 criticized the US for a policy of 'containment, encirclement and suppression of China, which has bought unprecedented severe challenges to our country's development'.[18] These comments point to the belief among Chinese leadership that disputes over human rights, democratic values, rule of law and international norms have deliberately been stoked to make trouble to demonize and contain China, and in response China needs to consolidate its own power to counter this. China's nuclear policy is part of a broader drive to modernize the entire Chinese military, investing in new forms of conventional weaponry as well. This is also reflective of a drive to promote national pride and technological prowess.

The Biden administration's National Security Strategy in 2022 identified that:

> Our competitors and potential adversaries are investing heavily in new nuclear weapons. By the 2030's, the United States for the first time will need to deter two major nuclear

> powers, each of whom will field modern and diverse global and regional nuclear forces. To ensure our nuclear deterrent remains responsive to the threats we face, we are modernizing the nuclear Triad, nuclear command and control, and communications, and our nuclear weapons infrastructure, as well as strengthening our deterrence commitments to our allies.[19]

The US is expected to invest an estimated US$650 billion in modernizing all aspects of its programme.[20]

The UK has also committed to modernize its nuclear programme. Having pledged in 2010 to reduce the size of its overall nuclear stockpile by 65 per cent, it has since raised the cap to no more than 260 warheads.[21] The estimated cost of replacing the UK's design and manufacture of four nuclear submarines is £31 billion.[22] A £10 billion contingency has also been set aside, making a potential spend of £41 billion.[23] As of March 2023, 20% of the contingency had been accessed so far.[24] France is also investing in modernizing its nuclear programme to upgrade its submarine-launched missiles and air force capabilities, with a budget of €37 billion for 2018–25.[25]

The challenge with these modernization programmes is that they change the possibility of conflict and use. Tactical nuclear weapons, no matter how small, are still nuclear weapons and still cause environmental and human destruction. However, are there circumstances in which a small-scale, limited use of nuclear weapons might be deemed acceptable? We began this book, after all, looking at the decision to use them on Japanese cities in order to bring a six-year conflict to an end. I would argue that this is not the case; no matter how small these weapons become, they are still stigmatized due to their destructive nature and historical memory of their first use.

Nuclear symbolism today

In 2025, the strategic attraction of nuclear weapons remains. The international community is still concerned about Iran's enrichment of uranium and possible nuclear weapons programme. There is still the threat that more states will try to acquire nuclear weapons.

Converting a nuclear energy programme into a military one is time-consuming and extremely challenging. Previous chapters have documented this. While it has no plans to develop nuclear weapons and is a member of the Treaty on the Non-Proliferation of Nuclear Weapons, Japan has the expertise, capital and technology to convert its nuclear energy programme into a weapons programme. Japan has had an extended deterrence agreement with the US since 1951. Despite this, it has a highly sophisticated nuclear energy programme and large and sophisticated naval forces. It would seem highly unlikely that Japan, the only country to have experienced the effects of the use of nuclear weapons, would consider such an option. However, Japan's former president Shinzo Abe stated in February 2022, shortly after Russia's invasion of Ukraine, that 'Japan should consider a NATO-style nuclear-sharing arrangement'.[26] Japan has committed to spending

2 per cent of its GDP on its defence budget by 2027, a strategic shift for the country. Japan is responding to what it sees as a failure of deterrence to prevent the Russia–Ukraine War; Japanese strategists advocate increased spending to ensure increased 'resilience in infrastructure and readiness for sustained conflict'.[27]

The future for arms control: long live the taboo ...

So, where does this leave us today? What about the taboo? Have Russia's actions against Ukraine weakened it? Studies of European attitudes to nuclear weapons have highlighted increased public support. Over half of those surveyed in the Netherlands and Germany (two states stationing nuclear weapons) believed that nuclear weapons deter a nuclear attack. As this book goes to press, Poland has called for US nuclear weapons to be stationed on its soil as a deterrent to Russia. Support has also increased for the use of nuclear weapons as a second-strike capability and support for withdrawal of nuclear weapons has decreased. These studies highlight a shift in public opinion as a result of the increased threat from Russia.[28]

This is not to say that all is lost and the nuclear taboo is no longer valid. Russia's invasion of Ukraine has certainly highlighted the vulnerability of non-nuclear states to nuclear powers. It has also flagged up the importance of international cooperation and action. Opinion polls conducted in the UK after the outbreak of the Russia–Ukraine War found that, while the public is in favour of the UK possessing nuclear weapons, there is also continued support for efforts to control nuclear weapons and 39 per cent of the public would accept the UK joining the Treaty on the Prohibition of Nuclear Weapons.[29]

Interestingly, surveys of Russian public opinion after the invasion found 'a strong aversion'[30] to the use of nuclear weapons, which would indicate that, when war becomes a reality and the threat of nuclear use a possibility, the taboo strengthens.

All is not lost for nuclear disarmament either. The Treaty on the Prohibition of Nuclear Weapons is still gathering international support. In September 2024, Indonesia, the Solomon Islands and Sierra Leone signed the treaty. There are now 73 states parties to the treaty and 25 signatories.[31] Another sign of global commitment towards reducing the threat of nuclear weapons can be seen by the decision to award Nihon Hidankyo the 2024 Nobel Peace Prize. Nihon Hidankyo is an organization made up of the survivors of the atomic bomb attacks on Hiroshima and Nagasaki. The organization, and its members, the *Hibakusha*, travel around the world providing personal testimonies of their experiences on the day of the nuclear attacks.[32] Groups such as Nihon Hidankyo remind the world of the abhorrent reality of nuclear weapons.

This book has tried to show that nuclear weapons are unique due to their strategic, political and moral quality. Do nuclear weapons make the world a safer place? As long as nuclear weapons exist, there also exists the need for the international community to work together to find ways to prevent their spread and ultimately to work to prevent conflict. Nuclear weapons are a reminder of the horrors of war, but also of the importance of the preservation of humanity and peace. For now, this is what nuclear weapons are for.

NOTES

Chapter 1

1. The Bulletin of the Atomic Scientists, 'Doomsday Clock', https://thebulletin.org/doomsday-clock/
2. 'Megumi Shinoda, Eyewitness Testimony', *Project 1945*, https://www.1945project.com/portfolio-item/megumi-shinoda/#1498206302968-41dc96a7-7877
3. Atomic Heritage Foundation, 'Little Boy and Fat Man: Bombings of Hiroshima and Nagasaki', 23 July 2014, https://ahf.nuclearmuseum.org/ahf/history/little-boy-and-fat-man/
4. 'Yasujiro Tanaka, Eyewitness Testimony', *Project 1945*, https://www.1945project.com/portfolio-item/yasujiro-tanaka/#1498206243077-a2c63dfd-b1ed
5. Atomic Heritage Foundation, 'Survivors of Hiroshima and Nagasaki', 27 July 2017, https://ahf.nuclearmuseum.org/ahf/history/survivors-hiroshima-and-nagasaki/
6. Atomic Archive.com, 'The Atomic Bombings of Hiroshima and Nagasaki', https://www.atomicarchive.com/resources/documents/med/med_chp10.html
7. For further information please see: The Harry S. Truman Library Archives, 'Atomic Bomb: August 6, 1945', https://www.trumanlibrary.gov/education/lesson-plans/atomic-bomb-august-6-1945
8. The Army Historical Foundation, 'The M28/M29 Davy Crockett Nuclear Weapon System', https://armyhistory.org/the-m28m29-davy-crockett-nuclear-weapon-system/
9. Fabian Hoffmann and William Alberque, 'Non-Nuclear Weapons with Strategic Effect: New Tools of Warfare?', The International Institute for Strategic Studies, March 2022, https://www.iiss.org/research-paper/2022/03/non-nuclear-weapons-with-strategic-effect-new-tools-of-warfare/
10. Andrew Futter and Benjamin Zala, 'Strategic Non-Nuclear Weapons and the Onset of a Third Nuclear Age', *European Journal of International Relations*, 6, no. 1 (February 2021): 257–77.

Chapter 2

1. Gavin Thompson, Oliver Hawkins, Aliyah Dar and Mark Taylor, *Olympic Britain: Social and economic change since the 1908 and 1948 London Games* (UK House of Commons Library, 2012), p. 155, https://www.parliament.uk/contentassets/118c576e6da64ec68d8eebea5a09306b/olympicbritain.pdf
2. Toby Luckhurst, 'Dresden: The World War Two Bombing 75 Years On', *BBC*, 13 February 2020, http://bbc.co.uk/news/world-europe-51448486
3. See in Amit Roy, (2016) 'Story of Fission: Unlocking the Power of the Nucleus', *Resonance*, 21, (2016), pp. 247–58, https://doi.org/10.1007/s12045-016-0320-x
4. Atomic Heritage Foundation, 'Einstein-Szilard Letter', 2 August 1939, https://ahf.nuclearmuseum.org/ahf/key-documents/einstein-szilard-letter/
5. Paul Lawrence Rose, *Heisenberg and the Nazi Atomic Bomb Project: A Study in German Culture* (University of California Press, 1998), p. 11.
6. US Department of Energy, 'Background Information and Preservation Work', https://www.energy.gov/lm/manhattan-project-background-information-and-preservation-work
7. John D. Hart, 'The ALSOS Mission, 1943–1945: A Secret US Scientific Intelligence Unit', *International Journal of Intelligence and Counter-Intelligence*, 18, no. 3 (2005): 508–37 at p. 509.
8. Warren F. Kimball, 'The Atomic Bomb and the Special Relationship: Part 2', *The Churchill Project Hillsdale College*, 8 February 2022, https://winstonchurchill.hillsdale.edu/atomic-special-relationship/
9. Harry S. Truman National Archives, 'Handwriting on the Back of a Potsdam Photograph Describing Telling Stalin about the Atomic Bomb', 19 July 1945, 63-1456-46, https://www.trumanlibrary.gov/photograph-records/63-1456-46a
10. Barton J. Bernstein, 'Truman at Potsdam: His Secret Diary', *Presidential Studies Quarterly*, 29, no. 2 (1999): 488–9.
11. Atomic Archive, 'Leo Szilard's Petition to the President', 3 July 1945, https://www.atomicarchive.com/resources/documents/manhattan-project/szilard-petition.html
12. Office of the Historian, Department of the Army Files, No. 592, 'The Secretary of War (Stimson) to the President', Foreign Relations of the United States: Diplomatic Papers, The Conference of Berlin (The Potsdam Conference), 1945, Vol. 1, https://history.state.gov/historicaldocuments/frus1945Berlinv01/d592#:~:text=The%20

NOTES

Secretary%20of%20War%20(Stimson)%20to%20the%20 President%201&text=%5BWashington%2C%5D%20July%20 2%2C,have%20heretofore%20discussed%20with%20you

13 Atomic Archive, 'Order is Given', https://www.atomicarchive.com/history/atomic-bombing/hiroshima/page-5.html

14 Benjamin French, Sachiyo Funamoto, Hiromi Sugiyama, Ritsu Sakata, John Cologne, et al, 'Population Density in Hiroshima and Nagasaki before the Bombings in 1945: Its Measurement and Impact on Radiation Risk Estimates in the Life Span Study of Atomic Bomb Survivors', *American Journal of Epistemology*, 187, no. 8 (2018): 1623–9 at p. 1624.

15 Amy Briggs, 'Twists of Fate Made Nagasaki a Target 75 Years Ago', *National Geographic*, 5 August 2020, https://www.nationalgeographic.com/history/article/twists-fate-made-nagasaki-target-atomic-bomb

16 Atomic Science, 'Why Hiroshima?', https://www.atomicarchive.com/history/atomic-bombing/hiroshima/page-4.html

17 Mariko Oi, 'The Man Who Saved Kyoto from the Atomic Bomb', BBC News, 9 August 2015, https://www.bbc.co.uk/news/world-asia-33755182

18 Mariko Oi, 'The Man Who Saved Kyoto from the Atomic Bomb'.

19 National Archives: Harry S. Truman, 'Press Release by the White House', 6 August 1945, https://www.trumanlibrary.gov/library/research-files/press-release-white-house?documentid=NA&pagenumber=3

20 Manhattan Engineer District of the United States Army, 'The Atomic Bombings of Hiroshima and Nagasaki', Report, 29 June 1946, p. 6, https://www.atomicarchive.com/resources/documents/med/index.html

21 Atomic Heritage Foundation, 'Debate over the Bomb', 6 June 2014, https://ahf.nuclearmuseum.org/ahf/history/debate-over-bomb/

22 Michael J. Yavenditti, 'The American People and the Use of Atomic Bombs on Japan: The 1940s', *The Historian*, 36, no. 2 (February 1974): 224–247 at p. 232.

23 Rachel Cooke, 'Hiroshima by John Hersey: An enduring memory of reportage', *The Guardian*, 23 August 2016, https://www.theguardian.com/books/2016/aug/23/hiroshima-john-hersey-bomb-new-yorker-1946-enduring-reportage-rachel-cooke-shelf-life

24 Ian W. Toll, 'The Atomic Bombings by Ian W Toll', The National World War II Museum, New Orleans, 8 August 2020, https://www.nationalww2museum.org/war/articles/atomic-bombings-ian-w-toll

25 Jeremy Kuzmarov and Roger Peace, 'Was There a Diplomatic Alternative? The Atomic Bombing and Japan's Surrender', *The Asia Pacific Journal: Japan Version*, 19, issue 20, no. 4 (2021): Article 5643.
26 National Archives: Harry S. Truman Library, 'Kenneth McKellar to Harry S. Truman, Accompanied by a Report', 27 September 1945, p. 6, https://www.trumanlibrary.gov/library/research-files/kenneth-mckellar-harry-s-truman-accompanied-report?documentid=NA&pagenumber=2
27 National Archives, 'Kenneth McKellar to Harry S. Truman, Accompanied by a Report', p. 6.
28 Gregg Herken, 'A Most Deadly Illusion: The Atomic Secret and American Nuclear Weapons Policy, 1945–1950', *Pacific Historical Review*, 49, no. 1 (February 1980): 51–76 at p. 59.
29 The National Archives, 'The Iron Curtain Speech', 6 March 1946, Fulton, Missouri, USA, https://www.nationalarchives.gov.uk/education/resources/cold-war-on-file/iron-curtain-speech/
30 The National Archives, 'The Iron Curtain Speech'.

Chapter 3

1 Bernard Brodie, 'The Development of Nuclear Strategy', *International Security*, 2, no. 4 (Spring 1978): 65–83 at p. 65. First quoted in Bernard Brodie (ed), *The Absolute Weapon: Atomic Power and World Order* (Harcourt, Brace, 1946).
2 RG 59, Policy Planning Council Chronological Files, 1947–1962, box 1, Chronological 1949 National Security Archive Policy Document NN0760154. Policy Planning Staff: Question and Answer Session 21-22/9/1949, https://nsarchive.gwu.edu/document/19592-national-security-archive-doc-21-policy-planning (Questions 11 and 19).
3 Document NN0760154 (Question 20), p. 19.
4 Document NN0760154 (Question 20), p. 19.
5 Nicholas Wheeler, 'British Nuclear Weapons and Anglo–American Relations 1945–54', *International Affairs*, 61, no. 2 (1985–6): 71–86 at p. 73.
6 Office of the Historian, Milestones: 1945–1952, National Security Council paper NSC-68, https://history.state.gov/milestones/1945-1952/NSC68#:~:text=The%20authors%20of%20NSC%2D68%20rejected%20a%20renewal%20of%20U.S.,fend%20off%20further%20Soviet%20encroachments.

NOTES

7   US Government Spending.com, 'US Government Spending: Defence Spending since World War II', https://www.usgovernmentspending.com/defense_spending_history

8   Anne Harrington de Santana, 'Nuclear Weapons as the Currency of Power: Deconstructing the Fetishism of Force', *The Non-Proliferation Review*, 16, no. 3 (November 2009): 325–45 at p. 331.

9   Martin A. Smith, 'British Nuclear Weapons and NATO in the Cold War and Beyond', *International Affairs*, 87, no. 6 (November 2011): 1385–99 at p. 1387.

10   A.J.R. Groom, *British Thinking About Nuclear Weapons* (Pinter, 1974), p. 63.

11   Andrew M. Johnston, 'Mr Slessor Goes to Washington: The Influence of the British Global Strategy Paper on the Eisenhower New Look', *Diplomatic History*, 22 (1998): 361–98 at p. 369.

12   Beatrice Heuser, *NATO, Britain, France and the FRG: Nuclear Strategies and Forces for Europe, 1949–2000* (Macmillan Press, 1999), p. 17. Also see Jasen J. Castillo and Alexander B. Downes, 'Loyalty, Hedging, or Exit: How Weaker Alliance Partners Respond to the Rise of New Threats', *Journal of Strategic Studies*, 46, no. 2 (2023): 227–68 at p. 228.

13   Philippine de Lagausie, 'France's Nuclear-Weapons Policy: What's in it for Europe?', *International Centre for Defence and Security*, Commentary, 21 October 2022, https://icds.ee/en/frances-nuclear-weapons-policy-whats-in-it-for-europe/

14   Renny Babiarz, 'The People's Nuclear Weapon: Strategic Culture and the Development of China's Nuclear Weapons Program', *Comparative Strategy*, 34 (2015): 422–46 at p. 426.

Chapter 4

1   Patricia Shamai, 'Name and Shame: Unravelling the Stigmatization of Weapons of Mass Destruction', *Contemporary Security Policy*, 36, no. 1 (2015): 104–22.

2   Erving Goffman, *Stigma: Notes on the Management of Spoiled Identity* (Prentice-Hall, 1963).

3   William R. Slomanson, *Fundamental Perspectives on International Law* (West Publishing Company, 1996), p. 461.

4   Alva Myrdal, *The Game of Disarmament: How the United States and Russia Run the Arms Race* (Manchester University Press, 1977), p. 228.

5   Michael Walzer, *Just and Unjust Wars: A Moral Argument with Historical Illustrations*, 3rd edn (1977, reprint, Perseus Books Group, 2000), p. 21.

6   World Health Organization, 'Biological Weapons: Overview', https://www.who.int/health-topics/biological-weapons#tab=tab_1

7   Myrdal, *The Game of Disarmament*, p. 227.

8   Erhard Geissler and John Ellis van Courtland Moon (eds), *Biological and Toxic Weapons: Research, Development and Use from the Middle Ages to 1945* (Oxford University Press, 2000), p. 15.

9   Organisation for the Prohibition of Chemical Weapons (OPCW), 'What is a Chemical Weapon?', https://www.opcw.org/our-work/what-chemical-weapon#:~:text=A%20Chemical%20Weapon%20is%20a,the%20definition%20of%20chemical%20weapons

10   Myrdal, *The Game of Disarmament*, pp. 226–65.

11   George Bühler, *The Laws of Manu* (Oxford University Press, 1886), reprinted under UNESCO sponsorship as the *Sacred Books of the East*, Vol. 25 (Motilal Banarsidass, 1975), Internet Archive, at chapter 7, verse 90, https://archive.org/stream/mlbd.lawsofmanu0025unse_h6b1/mlbd.lawsofmanu0025unse_h6b1_djvu.txt

12   Robert Harris and Jeremy Paxman, *A Higher Form of Killing: The Secret History of Chemical and Biological Warfare* (Arrow Books, 2002), p. 1.

13   W. Seth Carus, 'Defining "Weapons of Mass Destruction"', *Centre for the Study of Weapons of Mass Destruction*, Occasional paper, no. 8 (National Defence University Press, 2012), p. 4.

14   Martha Finnemore and Kathryn Sikkink, 'International Norm Dynamics and Political Change', *International Organization*, 52, no. 4 (Autumn 1998): 887–917 at p. 891.

15   Nina Tannenwald, 'Stigmatizing the Bomb: Origins of the Nuclear Taboo', *International Security*, 29, no. 4 (Spring 2005): 5–49 at p. 8.

16   Tannenwald, 'Stigmatizing the Bomb', p. 11.

17   National Archives, Harry S. Truman Library, 'Statement by the President upon Signing the Federal Civil Defense Act of 1950', 12 January 1951, https://www.trumanlibrary.gov/library/public-papers/10/statement-president-upon-signing-federal-civil-defense-act-1950

18   George Moore and Berwyn Moore, 'Threats to Our Nation, 1957–1959: A Public Health Retrospective', *Public Health Chronicles*, 124, no. 2 (2009): 323–7 at p. 324.

NOTES

19 Reba A. Wissner, 'TV and the Bomb', *Bulletin of the Atomic Scientists*, 13 August 2018, https://thebulletin.org/2018/08/tv-and-the-bomb/

20 Montgomery County Archives, Montgomery County Civil Defence Documents, 'Fallout Protection What to Know and Do About Nuclear Attack', 1961-12, 1999.008.B1.F3.002.04, https://cdm17128.contentdm.oclc.org/digital/collection/MCCivDefense/id/20/

21 Jonathan Hogg, *British Nuclear Culture: Official and Unofficial Narratives in the Long 20th Century* (Bloomsbury, 2016), p. 81.

22 Amelia Tait, '"When You Hear the Four-minute Warning" ... Whatever Happened to Britain's Nuclear Bunkers?', *The Guardian*, 24 November 2022, https://www.theguardian.com/world/2022/nov/24/when-you-hear-the-four-minute-warning-whatever-happened-to-britains-nuclear-bunkers

23 Jeff Hughes, 'The Strath Report: Britain Confronts the H-Bomb, 1954–55', *History and Technology*, 19, no. 3 (2003): 257–75 at p. 257.

24 Winston Churchill, 'The Hydrogen Bomb: Churchill's Last Major Speech in Parliament', 1 March 1955, *Hansard*, 5th Series, Volume 537, cc 1893, https://www.parliament.uk/about/living-heritage/transformingsociety/private-lives/yourcountry/collections/churchillexhibition/churchill-the-orator/hydrogen/

25 Jack Niedenthal, 'A Short Story of the People of Bikini Atoll', https://marshall.csu.edu.au/Marshalls/html/History_Varia/Bikini_History/Bikini_History.html

26 *JSTOR*, 'Shared Collections: Bombs and the Bikini Atoll', https://daily.jstor.org/bombs-and-the-bikini-atoll/

27 'The World on the Brink: John F. Kennedy and the Cuban Missile Crisis: Day 3, October 18th', John F. Kennedy Presidential Library and Museum, https://microsites.jfklibrary.org/cmc/oct18/

28 Scott Sagan, 'Nuclear Alerts and Crisis Management', *International Security*, 9, no. 4 (Spring 1985): 99–139 at p. 109.

29 'Radio and Television Report to the American People on the Soviet Arms Build-up in Cuba', John F. Kennedy Presidential Library and Museum, 22 October 1962, https://www.jfklibrary.org/archives/other-resources/john-f-kennedy-speeches/cuba-radio-and-television-report-19621022

30 Jonathan Colman, *The Cuban Missile Crisis: Origins, Course and Aftermath* (Edinburgh University Press, 2016), p. 94.

31 'Forty Years Ago: The Cuban Missile Crisis', *Prologue Magazine*, 34, no. 3 (Fall 2002), https://www.archives.gov/publications/prologue/2002/fall/cuban-missiles.html

Chapter 5

1. 'The Manhattan Project: Making the Atomic Bomb', Part VI, The Manhattan District in Peacetime: The Baruch Plan, *Atomic Archives.com*, https://www.atomicarchive.com/history/manhattan-project/p6s5.html
2. 'The Russian Bomb', *Daily Mail*, 24 September 1949.
3. Mohamed I. Shaker, *The Nuclear Non-Proliferation Treaty: Origin and Implementation 1959–1979*, vol. 1 (Oceana Publications, 1980), p. 11.
4. Natural Resources Defense Council records, MS 1965, Manuscripts and Archives, https://archives.yale.edu/repositories/12/resources/5167
5. 'Text of Speech by the Minister for External Affairs Mr Frank Aiken T.D in the First (Political) Committee of the UN', https://www.dfa.ie/media/dfa/alldfawebsitemedia/ourrolesandpolicies/disarmament-frank-aiken-speech-1958.pdf
6. 'Text of Speech by the Minister for External Affairs Mr Frank Aiken T.D in the First (Political) Committee of the UN'.
7. Lauren Barbour, 'Fissile Material Cutoff Treaty: A Chronology', Institute for Science and International Security, https://isis-online.org/publications/fmct/chronology.html
8. International Atomic Energy Agency, 'Atoms for Peace Speech', 8 December 1953, https://www.iaea.org/about/history/atoms-for-peace-speech
9. John Simpson, Kristan Stoddard and Marion Swinerd, 'Nuclear Weapons: An Introductory Guide: Part 1', MCIS CNS NPT Briefing Book, Mountbatten Centre for International Studies (University of Southampton: 2009), p. 4.
10. Nina Tannenwald, *The Nuclear Taboo: The United States and the Non-Use of Nuclear Weapons Since 1945* (Cambridge University Press, 2007), p. 161.
11. Alison Kraft, 'Dissenting Scientists in Early Cold War Britain: The "Fallout" Controversy and the Origins of Pugwash, 1954–1957', *Journal of Cold War Studies*, 20, no. 1 (Winter 2018): 58–100.
12. Paul Boyer, 'From Activism to Apathy: The American People and Nuclear Weapons, 1963–1980', *The Journal of American History*, 70, no. 4 (March 1984): 821–44 at p. 822.

NOTES

13. The Martin Luther King, Jr. Research and Education Institute, Stanford, 'National Committee for a Sane Nuclear Policy (SANE)', 22 April 1957, http://kinginstitute.stanford.edu/national-committee-sane-nuclear-policy-sane
14. Josef Joffee, 'Peace and Populism: Why the European Anti-Nuclear Movement Failed', *International Security*, 11, no. 4 (Spring 1987): 3–40 at p. 14.
15. Kate Hudson Blog, 'How Bruce Kent led CND in the 80s', Campaign for Nuclear Disarmament, 12 June 2022, http://cnduk.org/how-bruce-kent-led-cnd-in-the-80s/
16. Janet W. Schofield and Mark A. Pavelchak, 'Fallout from *The Day After*: The Impact of a TV Film on Attitudes Related to Nuclear War', *Journal of Applied Social Psychology*, 19, no. 5 (April 1989): 433–48.
17. Susan T. Fiske, Felicia Pratto and Mark A. Pavelchak, 'Citizens' Images of Nuclear War: Content and Consequences', *Journal of Social Issues*, 39, Issue 1 (Spring 1983): 41–65.
18. Christian Joppke, 'Social Movements During Cycles of Issue Attention: The Decline of the Anti-Nuclear Energy Movements in West Germany and the USA', *The British Journal of Sociology*, 42, no. 1 (March 1991): 43–60 at p. 51.
19. Josef Joffee, 'Peace and Populism: Why the European Anti-Nuclear Movement Failed', *International Security*, 11, no. 4 (Spring 1987): 3–40 at p. 36.
20. European Commission, International Atomic Energy Agency and World Health Organization, *One Decade after Chernobyl: Summing Up the Consequences of the Accident*, proceedings of an international conference, 8–12 April 1986 (IAEA, 1986), p. 7.
21. Richard Gray, 'The True Toll of the Chernobyl Disaster', *BBC*, 26 July 2019, https://www.bbc.com/future/article/20190725-will-we-ever-know-chernobyls-true-death-toll

Chapter 6
1. George H.W. Bush, 'Address Before a Joint Session of the Congress on the State of the Union', George H.W. Bush Presidential Library & Museum, 29 January 1991, https://bush41library.tamu.edu/archives/public-papers/2656
2. Bush, 'Address Before a Joint Session of the Congress on the State of the Union'.
3. Francis Fukuyama, 'The End of History', *National Interest*, no. 16 (Summer 1989): 3–18 at p. 4.

4   Fukuyama, 'The End of History', p. 18.
5   Graham Allison, 'What Happened to the Soviet Superpower's Nuclear Arsenal? Clues for the Nuclear Security Summit', Harvard Kennedy School Faculty Research Working Paper Series, No. RWP12-038, August 2012, https://www.hks.harvard.edu/publications/what-happened-soviet-superpowers-nuclear-arsenal-clues-nuclear-security-summit
6   Jason Ellis, 'Nunn-Lugar's Mid-Life Crisis', *Survival*, 39, no. 1 (Spring 1997): 84–110 at p. 84.
7   Zondi Masiza, 'A Chronology of South Africa's Nuclear Program', *The Nonproliferation Review* (Fall 1993): 34–53 at p. 35.
8   William J. Long and Suzette R. Grillot, 'Ideas, Beliefs, and Nuclear Policies: The Cases of South Africa and Ukraine', *The Nonproliferation Review*, 7, no. 1 (Spring 2000): 24–40 at p. 24.
9   Aldo Zammit Borda, 'Ukraine War: What is the Budapest Memorandum and Why has Russia's Invasion Torn It Up?', *The Conversation*, 2 March 2022, https://theconversation.com/ukraine-war-what-is-the-budapest-memorandum-and-why-has-russias-invasion-torn-it-up-178184
10 Målfrid Braut-Hegghammer, 'Giving Up on the Bomb: Revisiting Libya's Decision to Dismantle its Nuclear Program', Wilson Centre Blog: Part of Middle Eastern History, 23 October 2017, https://www.wilsoncenter.org/blog-post/giving-the-bomb-revisiting-libyas-decision-to-dismantle-its-nuclear-program
11 Susan J. Koch, *Case Study Series: The Presidential Nuclear Initiatives of 1991–1992* (National Defence University Press, 2012).
12 Ivo H. Daalder, 'NATO's Purpose After the Cold War', chapter 1 of 'NATO in the 21st Century: What Purpose? What Missions?', Brookings Institution, 1 April 1999, p. 6, www.brookings.edu/articles/nato-in-the-21st-century-what-purpose-what-missions/
13 Julian Borger, 'The Truth about Israel's Secret Nuclear Arsenal', *The Guardian*, 15 January 2014, https://www.theguardian.com/world/2014/jan/15/truth-israels-secret-nuclear-arsenal
14 William J. Broad and David E. Sanger, '"Last Secret" of 1967 War: Israel's Doomsday Plan for Nuclear Display', *The New York Times*, 3 June 2017, http://nytimes.com/2017/06/03/world/middleeast/1967-arab-israeli-war-nuclear-warning.html
15 United Nations, 'The Question of Palestine 'Israeli Nuclear Armament: Report of the Secretary General', https://www.un.org/unispal/document/auto-insert-184756/

NOTES

16. Arms Control Association, 'Nuclear Weapons: Who Has What at a Glance: Fact Sheets & Briefs, January 2025', *Arms Control Today*, https://www.armscontrol.org/factsheets/nuclear-weapons-who-has-what-glance
17. Arms Control Association, 'Nuclear Weapons'.
18. Hal Brands and David Palkki, 'Saddam, Israel, and the Bomb: Nuclear Alarmism Justified?', *International Security*, 36, no. 1 (Summer 2011): 133–66 at p. 133.
19. Brands and Palkki, 'Saddam, Israel, and the Bomb', p. 146.
20. Richard L. Russell, 'Iraq's Chemical Weapons Legacy: What Others Might Learn from Saddam', *Middle East Journal*, 59, no. 2 (Spring 2005): 187–208 at p. 194.
21. Miller Centre, 'Statecraft: The Bush 41 Team: The Gulf War', https://millercenter.org/statecraftmovie
22. Brands and Palkki, 'Saddam, Israel, and the Bomb', p. 163.
23. Chietigj Bajpaee and Lisa Toremark, 'India-Russia Relations', *Chatham House*, http://chathamhouse.org/2024/10/india-russia-relations
24. National Security Archive, 'The US, Canada and Indian Nuclear Program, 1968–1974', https://nsarchive.gwu.edu/briefing-book/nuclear-vault/2022-12-09/us-canada-and-indian-nuclear-program-1968-1974
25. The Hindu Bureau, 'Watch: 50 Years Ago, India Conducted its First Nuclear Test', *The Hindu*, 18 May 2024, https://www.thehindu.com/news/national/watch-50-years-ago-india-conducted-its-first-ever-nuclear-test/article68187908.ece
26. *BBC News*, 'AB Vajpayee: The PM Who Consolidated India as a Nuclear Power', 16 August 2018, https://www.bbc.co.uk/news/world-south-asia-25123943
27. Qamar Shahzad, 'What's in a Name? The Etymology of South Asia's Missiles', *Defence and Security, Nuclear Issues*, 29 February 2024, https://southasianvoices.org/nuc-m-pk-n-etymology-of-south-asias-missiles-02-29-2024/
28. *BBC News*, 'World: Monitoring Nawaz Sharif's Speech', 28 May 1998, http://news.bbc.co.uk/1/hi/world/monitoring/102445.stm

Chapter 7

1. Bruce Hoffman, 'Rethinking Terrorism and Counterterrorism since 9/11', *Studies in Conflict and Terrorism*, 25 (2002): 303–16 at p. 304.

2   Bruce Hoffman, 'Rethinking Terrorism and Counterterrorism since 9/11', p. 313.
3   'Remarks by President Barack Obama in Prague as Delivered', *The White House Office of the Press*, 5 April 2009, https://obama whitehouse.archives.gov/the-press-office/remarks-president-barack-obama-prague-delivered
4   Ewen MacAskilll and Julian Borger, 'Iraq War was Illegal and Breached UN Charter, Says Annan', *The Guardian*, 16 September 2004, https://www.theguardian.com/world/2004/sep/16/iraq.iraq
5   *History*, 'This Day in History: Millions Protest the Impending Invasion of Iraq', 15 February 2003, https://www.history.com/this-day-in-history/millions-protest-iraq-war-february-15
6   Michael E. O'Hanlon, 'Saddam's Bomb: How Close is Iraq to Having a Nuclear Weapon?', The Brookings Institution, 18 September 2002, https://www.brookings.edu/articles/saddams-bomb-how-close-is-iraq-to-having-a-nuclear-weapon/
7   Sanchia Berg, 'Tony Blair was Warned of "Appalling" Attack on UK after 9/11', *BBC News*, 19 July 2003, https://www.bbc.co.uk/news/uk-66233974
8   United Nations, 'UN Security Council Resolution 1540 (2004)', https://disarmament.unoda.org/wmd/sc1540/
9   Dan Zak, '"Nothing Ever Ends": Sorting through Rumsfeld's Knowns and Unknowns', *Washington Post*, 1 July 2021, https://www.washingtonpost.com/lifestyle/style/rumsfeld-dead-words-known-unknowns/2021/07/01/831175c2-d9df-11eb-bb9e-70fda8c37057_story.html
10   Gareth Porter, 'When the Ayatollah Said No to Nukes', *Foreign Policy*, 16 October 2014, https://foreignpolicy.com/2014/10/16/when-the-ayatollah-said-no-to-nukes/
11   Khosro Sayeh Isfahani, 'The Nuclear Fatwa That Wasn't – How Iran Sold the World a False Narrative', *Atlantic Council*, 9 May 2024, https://www.atlanticcouncil.org/blogs/iransource/iran-nuclear-weapons-fatwa-khamenei/
12   *NBC News: Associated Press*, 'Iran Asserts Right to Enrich Uranium', 15 September 2004, https://www.nbcnews.com/id/wbna6012416
13   Emma Hurd, 'Iran Lashes Out at "Little Satan" Britain', *Sky News*, 30 November 2011, https://news.sky.com/story/iran-lashes-out-at-little-satan-britain-10483414

NOTES

14. Arms Control Association, 'Background and Status of Iran's Nuclear Program', https://www.armscontrol.org/research-reports/2014-06/section-1-background-status-irans-nuclear-program
15. Isfahani, 'The Nuclear Fatwa That Wasn't'.
16. Claire Mills, 'What is the Status of Iran's Nuclear Programme and the JCPOA?', House of Commons Library, 4 October 2024, https://commonslibrary.parliament.uk/research-briefings/cbp-9870/
17. Mills, 'What is the Status of Iran's Nuclear Programme and the JCPOA?'.
18. Claire Mills and John Curtis, 'Israel–Iran 2025: Developments in Iran's nuclear programme and military action', House of Commons Library Research Briefing, No. 10284, 24 June 2025, pp. 2–45 at p. 3.
19. Alexandre Y. Mansourov, 'The Origins, Evolution, and Current Politics of the North Korean Nuclear Program', *The Nonproliferation Review*, 2, no. 3 (Spring–Summer 1995): 25–38 at p. 30.
20. Andrew Mack, 'North Korea and the Bomb', *Foreign Policy*, no. 83 (Summer 1991): 87–104 at p. 89.
21. Grace Lee, 'The Political Philosophy of Juche', *Time Magazine*, 3, no. 1 (Spring 2003): 105–12 at p. 105.
22. *The Guardian*, 'North Korea Withdraws from Nuclear Treaty', 10 January 2003, https://www.theguardian.com/world/2003/jan/10/northkorea1
23. Andrew Natsios, 'The Politics of Famine in North Korea', United States Institute of Peace website, 2 August 1999, https://www.usip.org/publications/1999/08/politics-famine-north-korea
24. Barack Obama, 'Remarks to the Chicago Council on Global Affairs', The American Presidency Project, http://www.presidency.ucsb.edu/documents/remarks-the-chicago-council-global-affairs
25. Obama, 'Remarks to the Chicago Council on Global Affairs'.
26. Daryl G. Kimball, 'A Perilous Precedent', *Arms Control Today*, 1 April 2003, http://armscontrol.org/act/2003-04/focus/perilous-precedent
27. 'Remarks by President Barack Obama in Prague', *The White House Office of the Press*.
28. World Nuclear Association, 'Safety of Nuclear Reactors', 11 February 2025, https://world-nuclear.org/information-library/safety-and-security/safety-of-plants/safety-of-nuclear-power-reactors#:~:text=Fukushima%20Daiichi%20(Japan%202011)%20where,were%20killed%20by%20the%20tsunami

29. ICAN website, https://www.icanw.org/
30. Tom Sauer and Mathias Reveraert, 'The Potential Stigmatizing Effect of the Treaty on the Prohibition of Nuclear Weapons', *Nonproliferation Review*, 25, no. 5–6 (2018): 437–55 at p. 442.
31. Linh Schroeder, 'The ICRC and the Red Cross and Red Crescent Movement: Working towards a Nuclear-Free World Since 1945', *Journal for Peace and Nuclear Disarmament*, 1, no. 1 (2018): 66–78 at p. 70.
32. ICAN, 'The Campaign', https://www.icanw.org/the_campaign

Chapter 8

1. Rishi Paul, 'Bluff and Bluster: Why Putin Revised Russia's Nuclear Doctrine', *European Leadership Network*, 25 November 2024, http://europeanleadershipnetwork.org/commentary/bluff-and-bluster-why-putin-revised-russias-nuclear-doctrine
2. CSIS, Project on Nuclear Issues, 'Nuclear Signaling During the War in Ukraine', https://nuclearrussiaukraine.csis.org/#about
3. Heather Williams, 'Why Russia is Changing its Nuclear Doctrine Now', CSIS, 27 September 2024, https://www.csis.org/analysis/why-russia-changing-its-nuclear-doctrine-now
4. Frances Mao, 'Putin Proposes New Rules for Using Nuclear Weapons', *BBC*, 25 September 2024, https://www.bbc.co.uk/news/articles/c5yjej0rvw0o
5. Jeremy Straub, 'A Cyberattack Could Wreak Destruction Comparable to a Nuclear Weapon', *The Conversation*, 16 August 2019, https://theconversation.com/a-cyberattack-could-wreak-destruction-comparable-to-a-nuclear-weapon-112173
6. Washington State Department of Health, 'Electromagnetic Pulse (EMP), Fact Sheet', Division of Environmental Health, Office of Radiation Protection, 320-090, September 2003, https://doh.wa.gov/sites/default/files/legacy/Documents/Pubs/320-090_elecpuls_fs.pdf
7. The White House, 'Briefing Room Statement, Joint Statement of the Leaders of the Five Nuclear-Weapon States on Preventing Nuclear War and Avoiding Arms Races', 3 January 2022, https://bidenwhitehouse.archives.gov/briefing-room/statements-releases/2022/01/03/p5-statement-on-preventing-nuclear-war-and-avoiding-arms-races/
8. SIPRI, 'Role of Nuclear Weapons Grows as Geopolitical Relations Deteriorate: New SIPRI Yearbook Out Now', 17 June 2024, https://www.sipri.org/media/press-release/2024/role-nuclear-weapons-grows-geopolitical-relations-deteriorate-new-sipri-

yearbook-out-now#:~:text='While%20the%20global%20total%20of,said%20SIPRI%20Director%20Dan%20Smith

9 Hans Kristensen, 'How Presidents Arm and Disarm', Global Risk, Federation of American Scientists, https://fas.org/publication/stockpilereductions/

10 Hans Kristensen, Matt Korda, Eliana Johns, Mackenzie Knight-Boyle and Kate Kohn, 'Status of World Nuclear Forces', http://fas.org/initiative/status-world-nuclear-forces

11 Robert S. Norris and Hans M. Kristensen, 'The British Nuclear Stockpile 1953–2013', *Bulletin of Atomic Sciences*, 69, no. 4 (2013): 69–75 at p. 69.

12 Claire Mills, 'Nuclear Weapons at a Glance: United Kingdom', House of Commons Library Research Briefing, No. 9077, 1 August 2024, pp. 4–18.

13 Hans M. Kristensen, 'II. Russian Nuclear Forces' in *SIPRI Yearbook 2014: Armament, Disarmament and National Security* (SIPRI, 2014), pp. 299–308, https://www.sipri.org/sites/default/files/SIPRIYB14c06sII.pdf

14 Hans M. Kristensen, Matt Korda, Eliana Johns, Mackenzie Knight-Boyle and Kate Kohn, 'Global Risk: Status of World Nuclear Forces', Federation of American Scientists (FAS), 26 March 2025, https://fas.org/initiative/status-world-nuclear-forces/

15 Hans M. Kristensen, Matt Korda, Eliana Johns and Mackenzie Knight, 'Indian Nuclear Weapons, 2024', Nuclear Notebook, *Bulletin of the Atomic Scientists*, 80, no. 5 (2024): 326–42.

16 Naeem Salik, 'Pakistan's Nuclear Force Structure in 2025', *Carnegie Endowment for International Peace*, 30 June 2016, https://carnegieendowment.org/research/2016/06/pakistans-nuclear-force-structure-in-2025?lang=en

17 Hans M. Kristensen, Matt Korda, Eliana Johns and Mackenzie Knight, 'Chinese Nuclear Weapons 2025', *Bulletin of the Atomic Scientists*, 12 March 2025, http://thebulletin.org/premium/2025-03/chinese-nuclear-weapons-2025/

18 Keith Bradsher, 'Xi Blames US "Containment" for Troubles Gripping China', *The New York Times*, 7 March 2023.

19 The White House, 'The Biden-Harris Administration's National Security Strategy', 12 October 2022, https://bidenwhitehouse.archives.gov/briefing-room/statements-releases/2022/10/12/fact-sheet-the-biden-harris-administrations-national-security-strategy/

20 Xiaodon Liang, 'US Nuclear Modernization Programs: Factsheets and Briefs', *Arms Control Association*, August 2024,

https://www.armscontrol.org/factsheets/us-modernization-2024-update#:~:text=The%20Pentagon%20spent%20more%20than,and%20improved%20accuracy%20and%20survivability

21 Mills, 'Nuclear Weapons at a Glance', p. 12.
22 Claire Mills and Esme Kirk-Wade, 'The Cost of the UK's Strategic Nuclear Deterrent', House of Commons Library Research Briefing, No. 8166, 22 August 2024, pp. 4–29 at p. 17.
23 Mills and Kirk-Wade, 'The Cost of the UK's Strategic Nuclear Deterrent', p. 5.
24 Mills and Kirk-Wade, 'The Cost of the UK's Strategic Nuclear Deterrent', p. 5.
25 Claire Mills, 'The French Nuclear Deterrent', House of Commons Library Research Briefing, No. 4079, 7 October 2020, pp. 3–24 at p. 23.
26 Sayuri Romei, 'Watching Ukraine, South Korea and Japan Eye Nuclear Weapons. Here's what the US should do.', *Bulletin of the Atomic Scientists*, 20 July 2023, https://thebulletin.org/2023/07/watching-ukraine-south-korea-and-japan-eye-nuclear-weapons-heres-what-the-us-should-do/
27 Daisuke Kawai, 'Japan's Defence Budget Surge: A New Security Paradigm', *Royal United Services Institute (RUSI)*, 2 December 2024, https://www.rusi.org/explore-our-research/publications/commentary/japans-defence-budget-surge-new-security-paradigm
28 Michal Onderco, Michal Smetana and Tom W. Etienne, 'Hawks in the Making? European Public Views on Nuclear Weapons, Post-Ukraine', *Global Policy*, 14, no. 2 (2023): 305–17 at p. 313.
29 '2023 UK Public Opinion Survey on Nuclear Weapons: Article and Data', *British Pugwash*, 9 May 2023, https://britishpugwash.org/2023-uk-public-opinion-survey-on-nuclear-weapons-article-and-data/
30 Michal Smetana and Michal Onderco, 'From Moscow with a Mushroom Cloud? Russian Public Attitudes to the Use of Nuclear Weapons in a Conflict with NATO', *Journal of Conflict Resolution*, 67, no. 2–3 (2022): 183–209.
31 ICAN, 'Why the Total Elimination of Nuclear Weapons Is More Urgent Than Ever on This International Day', 26 September 2024, https://www.icanw.org/why_the_total_elimination_of_nuclear_weapons_is_more_urgent_than_ever_on_this_international_day
32 Anna Lamche and James Landale, 'Japanese Atomic Bomb Survivors win Nobel Peace Prize', *BBC*, 11 October 2024, https://www.bbc.co.uk/news/articles/cy5y23qgx0qo

FURTHER READING

Books

Raymond Briggs, *When the Wind Blows* (Penguin Books, 1986).

Rhys Crilley, *Unparalleled Catastrophe: Life and Death in the Third Nuclear Age* (Manchester University Press, 2023).

John Hersey, *Hiroshima* (1946, reissued Penguin Books, 2002).

Fred Kaplan, *Wizards of Armageddon* (Stanford University Press, 1983).

Jeffrey Larsen and Kerry M. Kartchner, *On Limited Nuclear War in the 21st Century* (Stanford University Press, 2014).

Patricia Lewis, Heather Williams, Benoît Pelopidas and Sasan Aghlani, *Too Close for Comfort: Cases of Near Nuclear Use and Options for Policy* (Chatham House, 2014).

Maria Rost Rublee, *Nonproliferation Norms: Why States Choose Nuclear Restraint* (University of Georgia Press, 2009).

Nina Tannenwald, *The Nuclear Taboo: The United States and the Non-Use of Nuclear Weapons since 1945* (Cambridge University Press, 2007).

Films

Dr Strangelove or How I Learned To Stop Worrying and Love the Bomb (Stanley Kubrick, 1964).
Oppenheimer (Christopher Nolan, 2023).

Online resources

Arms Control Association: https://www.armscontrol.org/
BASIC: https://basicint.org/
Bulletin of the Atomic Scientists: https://thebulletin.org/
CSIS Project on Nuclear Issues: https://www.csis.org/programs/project-nuclear-issues
Fondation pour la recherche stratégique (The Foundation for Strategic Research, FRS): https://frstrategie.org/en/frs/presentation
Lowy Institute: https://www.lowyinstitute.org/about
Royal United Services Institute (RUSI): https://rusi.org/

INDEX

References to figures are in *italics*.

9/11 attacks 106–9
9/11 Commission 111

A
Abe, Shinzo 139
Advisory Committee on Uranium (US) 21
Ahmadinejad, Mahmoud 114
Aitken, Frank 72–3
Alberque, William 11–12
Al-Qaeda 106, 110
Alsos Mission (US) 23
Annan, Kofi 110
Anti-Ballistic Missile Treaty (1972) 77–8
anti-nuclear protests 69, 79–81, 82–4, *83*, 85–6, 124–5
see also campaign groups
arms race 38, 41–7, *43*
atomic bomb technology 6, 7
Atoms for Peace programme (US) 74–5, 112
Aum Shinrikyo 54
'Axis of Evil' 108

B
Baruch Plan (US) 70
Belarus 87
Berlin blockade 34–5
Berlin Wall 88–9
Biden, Joe 137–8
Bikini Atoll nuclear tests 50, 61–4, *62*, 79
biological weapons 53, 54
Blair, Tony 110
Borger, Julian 97–8
Boutros-Ghali, Boutros 89
Brodie, Bernard 13, 37–8
Budapest Memorandum 94
Bulletin of Atomic Scientists 1
Bush, George H.W. 89, 90, 95, 101, 133
Bush, George W. 108, 110, 120, 133

C
Campaign for Nuclear Disarmament 69, 84, 126
campaign groups 55, 69, 80–1, 84, 85–6, 125–7
Canada 23
Castro, Fidel 64
Catholic Church 52
Cat's Cradle (Vonnegut) 81
chemical weapons 20, 53–5, 100, 110, 114
Chernobyl accident 86–7
China 38, 41, 46–7, 76, 102, *121*, 136–7
Churchill, Winston 24, 25, 34, 44, 60
Civil Defence Corps (UK) 59

civil defence programmes 56–7, 59–61
Clinton, Bill 133
CNN 113
Cold War 9–10, 33–47, 68–70, 88–9, 90–2, 102–3, 116–17
Commoner, Barry 80
Comprehensive Test Ban Treaty (CTBT) 123
Co-operative Threat Reduction Programme (US) 93
cruise missiles 12
Cuban Missile Crisis 50–1, 64–6
cultural symbolism 15, 103
cyber attacks 11, 12, 131

D
Daily Mail 70–1
Davy Crockett Weapon System (US) 11
The Day After (film) 69, 85
The Day the Earth Caught Fire (film) 81
de Klerk, F.W. 94
decommissioning 13, 70, 93–5, 109, 133–5
détente 77–9
deterrence 12–13, 34–5, 37–8, 42, 44–5, 103
dirty bombs 93, 111
Doomsday clock 1
Dr Strangelove (film) 82
Dresden 20
drones 11, 12, 131
'Duck and Cover' campaign (US) 57–8

E
E-Bombs 132
Eden, Anthony 60
Egypt 97
Einstein, Albert 21
Eisenhower, Dwight D. 74–5

electromagnetic pulses (EMPs) 132
electronic warfare 12, 131–2

F
Federal Civil Defence Act (US) 57
Federation of American Scientists 69, 134, 136–7
First World War 20, 54–5
Fissile Material Cut-Off Treaty 68, 74, 123–4
fission bomb technology 6
France 23, 38, 45, 76, 97–8, 100, *121*, 138
Franck Report 33–4
Fuchs, Klaus 36
Fukushima accident 124–5
Fukuyama, Francis 90–1
fusion bomb technology 7–8, 10

G
Gaddafi, Muammar 94–5
Geneva Protocol 20, 54, 55
genocide 92
Germany 20, 21–2, 23, 24, 34–5, 85–6, 88–9, 140
Goffman, Erving 51
Gray, Richard 86
Greenglass, David 36
Greenpeace 69
'grey zone warfare' 129
Groves, General Leslie 23
Guardian 97–8
Gulf War 101–2

H
Hague Conventions 19–20
Hahn, Otto 20–1
Halsey, William, Jr 32
Hamburg 20
Harrington de Santana, Anne 42
heavy water 98, 113
Hersey, John 31

INDEX

Heuser, Beatrice 45
Hiroshima 1–3, *2*, 4–5, 28–32, 55
Hoffmann, Fabian 11–12
Hungary 88, 96
Hussein, Saddam 90, 99–100, 110
hypersonic missiles 12, 131

I

India 90, 100, 102–3, 104, *121*, 135
Innocent II, Pope 52
International Atomic Energy Agency (IAEA) 75, 76, 80, 86, 100, 102, 113, 116, 117
International Campaign to Abolish Nuclear Weapons 125–6
International Defense Review 99
international law 13–14, 19–20, 68, 76–8
International Physicians for the Prevention of Nuclear War 126
Iran 100, 108, 112–16, 129
Iran–Iraq War 100
Iraq 99–102, 108, 110–11
Iraq War 109, 110–12, 120
Israel 97–9, 116, *121*

J

Japan 1–5, *2*, 22, 24, 27, 28–31, 55, 124–5, 139–40, 141
Joffe, Josef 86
Johnson, Lyndon B. 74
Juche philosophy 118
Just War Theory 52–3

K

Kennedy, John F. 16, 50, 64, 65–6
Khamenei, Ali 113, 114

Khomeini, Ruhollah 113
Khrushchev, Nikita 46, 50, 66
Kim Il Sung 116, 117, 118
Kim Jong Il 118, 119
Kimball, Warren F. 24
kinetic weapons 12
Koran 52
Korean War 41, 117
Kuwait 100–1
Kyoto 28–9

L

Langer, William 33
Lapp, Ralph 80
Libya 90, 94–5
low-yield nuclear weapons 10, 11, 135–6, 138–9
Lugar, Richard 93

M

MacArthur, General Douglas 32
Manhattan Project 22–7, 32, 36
Mansourov, Alexandre 117
Manu Laws 54
Mao Zedong 46
McKellar, Kenneth 32–3
MIRV weapons (US) 10
Mohammad Reza Shah 112–13
morality *see* nuclear taboo; stigmatization
Mutually Assured Destruction (MAD) 38, 41, 42

N

Nagasaki 3–5, 28–9, 30–1, 55
nanotechnology 131
National Academy of Scientists (US) 80
National Committee for a Sane Nuclear Policy (US) 80–1
National Interest 90–1
Netherlands 140

New START Treaty (2011) 123, 134
New York Times 81, 98
New Yorker 31
Nihon Hidankyo 141
non-kinetic weapons 12
non-proliferation initiatives 13–14, 67–8, 71, 72–4, 76–8, 109, 119–24, 132–3
North Atlantic Treaty Organization (NATO) 10, 39, 45, 64, 82, 95–6, 130–1
North Korea 41, 108, 116–19, *121*
NPT (Treaty on the Non-Proliferation of Nuclear Weapons) (1970) 13–14, 68, 76–7, 90, 108, 109, 113, 117, 119, 126–7
nuclear accidents 86–7, 124–5
nuclear bomb technology 7–8, 10
nuclear bunkers 60–1
nuclear disarmament *see* decommissioning
nuclear energy 8–9, 14, 68, 74–5, 82, 86, 113–14, 124–5
nuclear fission 6, 6–7
nuclear fusion 7, 10
nuclear modernization programmes 11–12, 129, 133–9
nuclear power *see* nuclear energy
nuclear powers 9
nuclear taboo 16, 49–51, 55–6, 129–30, 140–1
nuclear testing 46, 50, 61–4, *62*, 72, 79, 81, 90, 98–9, 103, 104, 108, 119, 123
nuclear warhead stockpiles *43*, 93, *121*, 133–8
Nunn, Sam 93
Nunn May, Alan 36

O

Obama, Barack 109, 119–23, 124, 133, 134
Old Testament 52
On the Beach (Shute) 81
Operation Desert Storm 101
The Outer Limits (TV series) 81

P

Pakistan 90, 102, 104, *121*, 135
Partial Test Ban Treaty (1963) 73, 81, 123
Partnership for Peace (NATO) 96
Pauling, Linus 81
Pepper, Claude 33
Poland 88, 96, 140
Pontecorvo, Bruno 36
Potsdam Conference 25–6, 27
Prithviraj Chauhan 103
public awareness campaigns 56–61
public opinion 55–6, 140–1
 see also nuclear taboo; public protests
public protests 69, 79–81, 82–4, *83*, 85–6
 see also campaign groups
Pugwash movement 81
Putin, Vladimir 130

R

radiation poisoning 3–4, 8, 63, 80, 86–7
Reagan, Ronald 16
Red Alert (TV film) 82
Responsibility to Protect doctrine (UN) 92
Roosevelt, Franklin D. 21, 25
Rosenberg, Julius and Ethel 36
Rouhani, Hassan 115

INDEX

Royal Observer Corps (UK) 59–60, 61
Rumsfeld, Donald 112
Russia 11, 13, *121*, 123, 128–9, 130–1, 134–5, 136, *136*
see also Soviet Union
Russia–Ukraine War 11, 128–9, 130–1
Rwanda 92

S

Safeguard programme (US) 77
Saracens 52
satellite technology systems 131–2
Schelling, Thomas 16
Science (journal) 80
Second World War 1–5, *2*, 18–19, 20, 22–3, 24, 28–30, 55
Sentinel programme (US) 77
Sharif, Nawaz 104
Shigemitsu, Mamoru 5
Sino-Soviet Treaty (1950) 46
Six-Day War 98, 100
Smith, Dan 133
South Africa 13, 90, 94, 99
South Korea 117–18
Soviet Union 9–10, 19, 25, 27, 30, 33–6, 39, 40, 41, *43*, 44, 46, 50–1, 58, 64–6, 70–1, 73, 76, 77–8, 92–3, 100, 102–3, 116–17, 117–18
space technology 44
Spartans 53–4
splitting the atom 6–7, 20–1
St Louis Committee for Nuclear Information 80
Stalin, Joseph 25, 30, 33, 34, 35
Stewart, Alice 80
stigmatization 51–6
Stimson, Henry 27, 29
Strassmann, Fritz 20–1
Strategic Arms Limitation Talks (SALT) 78–9
Strategic Arms Reduction Treaty (2011) 123, 134
strategic value 12–13, 37–9, 41, 44–5, 90, 118–19
see also deterrence
Strath Report (UK) 60
Strontium-90 80
Suez Crisis 97
symbolic value 15, 95, 103, 139–40
Szilard, Leo 21

T

tactical nuclear weapons 10, 11, 135–6, 138–9
Tannenwald, Nina 56, 79
terrorism 106–9, 111–12
Thatcher, Margaret 95, 101
Thomas Aquinas, Saint 52
Threads (film) 85
Three Mile Island accident 86
Treaty on the Non-Proliferation of Nuclear Weapons (1970) (NPT) 13–14, 68, 76–7, 90, 108, 109, 113, 117, 119, 126–7
Treaty on the Prohibition of Nuclear Weapons (2021) 109, 127, 141
Trident submarine system (UK) 134, 138
Truman, Harry S. 1, 25, 26, 27, 35
Trump, Donald 115, 129–30, 136
'Tsar Bomb' (Soviet Union) 10
Twilight Zone (TV series) 81

U

Ukraine 11, 13, 86–7, 90, 94, 128–9, 130–1
Umezu, General Yoshijiro 5

United Kingdom 20, 22–3, 24, 25, 32, 38, 44–5, 59–61, 73, 76, 97, 110, *121*, 134, 138, 140–1
United Kingdom Warning and Monitoring Organisation 61
United Nations 39, 55, 66, 87, 89, 94
United Nations General Assembly 72–3, 74–5, 92, 124, 127
United Nations Security Council 38, 101, 110, 111–12
United States 1–5, *2*, 10, 22–7, 28–33, 34–5, 37–8, 39–42, *43*, 50–1, 56–9, 61–6, *62*, 67–8, 70, 72, 73, 74–5, 76, 77–8, 93–4, *95*, 101, 102, 106, 107–8, 110–11, 112–13, 114, 115–16, 117, 119–23, *121*, 124, 130–1, 133–4, 136, 137–8
uranium 8, 20–1, 71–2, 113, 116, 117

V
Vandenberg, Arthur H. 33

W
Wagner, Robert F. 33
The War Game (drama-documentary) 81–2
Warsaw Pact 39
Watkins, Peter 81–2
Weapons of Mass Destruction, use of term 55, 108, 110
When the Wind Blows (film) 69, 84–5
White Sands missile tests 23–4
Women's International League for Peace and Freedom 55, 126
World Trade Center 106

X
Xi Jinping 137

Y
Yalta Conference 25
Ypres, Second Battle of 54

Z
Zammit Borda, Aldo 94

www.ingramcontent.com/pod-product-compliance
Lightning Source LLC
Chambersburg PA
CBHW020413080526
44584CB00014B/1313